YOUR A to Z OF RESEARCH METHODS AND STATISTICS IN PSYCHOLOGY

T0347606

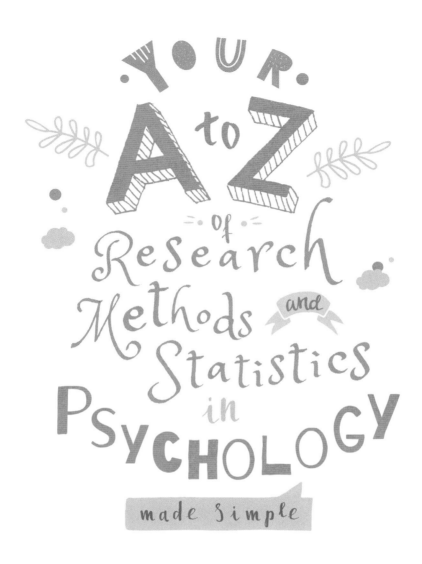

YOUR A to Z of Research Methods and Statistics in Psychology

made simple

BARBARA KINGSLEY and JULIA ROBERTSON

BUCKINGHAMSHIRE NEW UNIVERSITY

OXFORD
UNIVERSITY PRESS

OXFORD
UNIVERSITY PRESS

Great Clarendon Street, Oxford, OX2 6DP,
United Kingdom

Oxford University Press is a department of the University of Oxford.
It furthers the University's objective of excellence in research, scholarship,
and education by publishing worldwide. Oxford is a registered trade mark of
Oxford University Press in the UK and in certain other countries

Published in the United States of America by Oxford University Press
198 Madison Avenue, New York, NY 10016, United States of America

British Library Cataloguing in Publication Data
Data available

Library of Congress Control Number: 2020932173

ISBN 978–0–19–881294–4

Printed in Great Britain by
Bell & Bain Ltd., Glasgow

For these special people—George and Arlo, Anna, Katy and Amy.

ACKNOWLEDGEMENTS

We would firstly like to say a huge thank you to Martha Bailes for all her support and encouragement throughout the writing of this book. Her input has always been valuable, tactful (a real master!) and humorous—and our working lunches have always been something to look forward to!

We would also like to thank the various academics and students who have reviewed our book with insight and understanding as we have progressed—their comments have been much appreciated.

And lastly, we would like to thank our students, not only for showing at least some enjoyment in our classes, but also for their 'Student Says' contributions. Although some of these have developed over time, many have been inspired by students past and present and we would like to thank them all for their valued input!

Please note that, as they are provided for purely illustrative purposes, not all tables and figures follow APA style formatting. When producing your own tables and figures, please refer to your institutional guidelines on how these should be presented.

a-priori comparisons When we look at the differences between several groups, there is sometimes a clear reason to assume that two particular groups are more likely to differ than any other pair of groups. The decision to look at that comparison before (*prior* to) conducting the experiment or getting the data is what is meant by an a priori comparison. An example is a study where the researcher wants to see how well participants perform on different memory tasks. They are presented with four different types of stimuli: words, numbers, faces, and patterns. While there could be differences between any pair of stimuli, it could be that, for example, words and faces are more likely to differ. So an a priori comparison between numbers and words is planned before the study starts. For this reason, it is also known as a '*planned comparison*'. You might be interested to know (OK, maybe not, but keep reading anyway . . .) that if you have an a priori prediction, the results of the primary analysis do not need to be significant for the comparison to be conducted (compare this to post hoc comparisons, which *do* need to be based on a significant result overall!)

Abstract (lab report) At some point in your psychology degree you will have the joy of writing a research report, and the abstract is a summary of the contents of that report. It will provide a concise summary of each section of the report—the *Literature review*, the *Methods section*, the *Results*, and the *Discussion*. Although written last, it appears at the start of the report and should enable the reader to decide whether they are interested in reading on (or not).

Acquiescence/Acquiescence bias An acquiescence bias is the tendency to agree with a statement or question whatever the content of it happens to be! This is known as 'yeah' saying. That might be because someone simply wants to be amiable (and agreeing with people is generally amiable) or it might be because the question is phrased in such a way that a positive response is invited (e.g. Did the birthday girl look pleased with her present?). If you want to avoid an acquiescence response bias you might prefer to use *open ended questions* in your *questionnaire* because they're more likely to encourage a more detailed, considered response.

Adjacency pair An adjacency pair is a term used in linguistics and *conversation analysis* which describes a part of conversation that requires or expects turn-taking. This would be between two individuals and would follow an expected protocol (procedure). For example, a first utterance (e.g. speech, a sound, an exclamation, etc.) could be the greeting and question—'Hello! How are you?'—with a second utterance expected to be a response to the greeting and an answer to the question (e.g. 'Hi! I'm good thanks!') If, on the other hand, you answered, 'It's raining outside', that would contravene the convention and would be sure to raise eyebrows!

Adjusted R^2 (Adjusted R squared) In regression analysis, R^2 tells us how much of the *variance* in the *criterion* (or *outcome*) *variable* is explained by the *predictor* variable(s) or, perhaps more simply, how well the analysis can predict changes in the criterion variable. By contrast, adjusted R^2 is a more conservative measure which accounts for the number of variables in the model. The more useless variables you add, the lower your adjusted R^2 will be. On the other hand, if you introduce useful, predictive variables, adjusted R^2 will increase. The reason for this (if you want to know!) is that R squared assumes that every predictor variable in the model explains the criterion variable (so every predictor variable you add will increase R^2), whereas adjusted R^2 actually recognizes the variation in only those variables which have, in reality, affected the criterion variable.

Alpha level (α) When we are conducting statistical tests we can never make any statement with 100% certainty because differences or relationships in the data we have collected *may* have occurred by chance. So, psychologists have to decide on how much chance to allow in order to accept that our results are *significant* (or have not occurred by chance). To do this they set what we call an alpha level. We might say, for example, that we should be 70% sure, or that we accept a 30% possibility that our results happened by chance (a .3 alpha level), or we might say that we should be 80% sure, or that we accept a 20% possibility that our results happened by chance (a .2 alpha level), etc. Actually in psychology we are pretty tough, and normal convention sets an alpha level of .05—in other words, we will only allow a 5% possibility that the result we obtained could have occurred by chance. Just occasionally, however, we need to set a more stringent alpha level (for example, in medical testing where you really don't want any error!), so we might set the alpha level at .01 (which would represent only a 1% possibility that our results happened by chance). See also *Significance level*.

Alpha reliability—see *Cronbach's alpha*

Alternate (or alternative) hypothesis—see *Experimental hypothesis*

Analysis of covariance (ANCOVA) This is an extension of *ANOVA* (you'll need to read about this first if you're not already clear about the ANOVA element of the ANCOVA), and is a procedure that allows us to control for the effects of one or more additional variables (*covariatesv*) that are not the direct focus of our study. These can be continuous or categorical. For example, if a researcher wanted to test the effect of a new drug (the *dependent variable*) in terms of age (young and old) and medical condition (chronic and acute), it would be important to know their participants' level of fitness prior to taking the new drug. So every group of participants (young chronic, young acute, old chronic, old acute) would each have their fitness measured, perhaps through heart rate, before the intervention was given, and this measure would then be the covariate, i.e. their initial fitness status would act as a benchmark for each individual, but would not be the main measure in the study. That said, if the covariate is significant it is telling us that level of fitness explains some variance in the DV. ANCOVA is often used in this type of pre-test/post-test experimental study.

Analysis of variance (ANOVA) This is a statistical technique that allows us to test the *significance* of the difference in the *means* (i.e. are they the same or not) between three or more groups (known as *levels*) in one *factor* (variable), or between the means of the groups in two or more factors at the same time (see Figure 1). The former is known as a *one-way ANOVA* and the latter a *factorial design* or *Factorial ANOVA*.

ANCOVA—see *Analysis of covariance*

Anomaly—see *Outlier*

Anonymity Anonymity is one of the ethical principles we need to consider when conducting research, and it relates to the identity of the participants. Providing anonymity means that any personal information that might identify participants is either not collected (e.g. names, email addresses, etc.), so there is nothing that can link a participant to their personal data (even the researcher would not be able to identify an individual participant), or is achieved when disseminating the research by changing the names of participants (using

Figure 1 Analysis of Variance (ANOVA)

Which ice cream do people prefer?

ONE-WAY ANOVA	One factor, 3 levels		Tests whether there is a significant difference in ice cream preference
FACTORIAL DESIGN	Two factors: Ice cream – vanilla, chocolate & strawberry Age group – children & adults	 and 	Tests three effects: whether there is a significant difference between ice cream preference, a significant difference between adults and children, and whether there is an interaction between the two.

pseudonyms) and locations (obscuring context), therefore protecting the identity of the individual.

ANOVA—see *Analysis of variance*

Apparatus (lab report) When you bake a cake you need to know the ingredients and the method used to bake it. Similarly, when you are writing up your research you need to describe your *Materials* (your cake-baking 'ingredients') and/or Apparatus (your cake-baking 'equipment'). The apparatus element of the *Method section* will specify exactly what equipment was used as well as the source of that equipment if commercially available (i.e. the manufacturer, make, and model). For example, a study investigating individual differences in learning behaviours in humans collected gaze data, the researchers stating, 'We recorded each participant's gaze movement . . . Using Tobii TX300 eye trackers connected to 23-inch monitors (Tobii Technology, Stockholm, Sweden)' (Toyokawa, Saito & Kameda, 2017, p.327). You will sometimes also see photos or images of the equipment used where this helps to visualize the equipment, though don't go overboard! Tempting though it may be to throw in loads of visual extras, if they *are* extras because they don't *really* add anything, they shouldn't be there!

Toyokawa, W., Saito, Y. & Kameda, T. (2017). Individual differences in learning behaviours in humans: Asocial exploration tendency does not predict reliance on social learning. *Evolution and Human Behavior*, 38(3), 325–33.

Appendix (lab report) The appendix (or plural, appendices/appendixes) is the section that comes at the end of a research report and which contains any supplementary information which you wouldn't normally put in the main body of the report. Essentially, this is additional information, as anything that is vital to understanding would appear in the report itself. An example might be the full list of items within a *questionnaire*, where only the title of the questionnaire has been referred to in the body of the report.

Applied research Unlike *pure research* which is interested in acquiring knowledge for the sake of knowledge itself, applied research is designed to solve particular problems of the world we live in. For example, a hospital might want to know how to encourage greater hand sanitation on the wards, so they might fund research which investigates this problem, perhaps designing some kind of intervention and assessing how well that intervention worked.

Archival research Archival research is so-named because it is research using 'archives' or existing records. For example, by researching the Utah Population Database, Moorad et al. (2011) found that with the outlawing in 1890 of polygynous marriage by Mormons (where one man could take on multiple wives), there has been reduced variation in the mating success of males in this group over the last century (so previously some men had many offspring and some had none whereas now most have one or two!).

Moorad, J.A., Promislow, D.E.L., Smith, K.R. & Wade, M.J. (2011). Mating system change reduces the strength of sexual selection in an American frontier population of the 19th century. *Evolution and Human Behavior*, 32(2), 147–55.

Association A statistical association can refer to two different things. It can simply be used to describe a *relationship* between two or

Figure 2 Asymptote

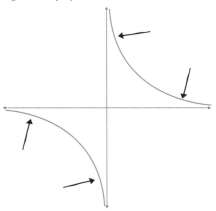

more *variables*. Alternatively, it can refer to the specific analyses that assess the degree to which differences in one variable are connected to differences in another, but importantly without inferring that one causes the other.

Asymptote An asymptote is a wonderful word that you can bandy around to show off when you need to. It refers to a curve on a graph as it approaches one of the axes and heads towards infinity, or, in other words, a curve that never quite touches the line, as in Figure 2. It can be vertical, horizontal, or oblique, and is of interest to us mostly when we are thinking about *distribution* in a *normal distribution curve*.

Attrition Attrition is when participants drop out of a study while the research is still ongoing and is therefore a particular issue in *longitudinal*

studies. There could be several reasons for this, e.g. moving to a different area, becoming ill, or just deciding they can't be bothered to take part any more! Losing participants from a study is problematic and could bias the results as the remaining sample may be less representative of the target population than was originally the case.

Audit trail An audit trail is a clear and detailed record of how a *qualitative* study was conducted. It would normally include all *field notes* as well as notes on any changes made in the research process along the way and the reasons for making those changes (although this, too, may be recorded in the field notes). A good audit trail is important in qualitative research as this sort of research tends to be iterative (by which we mean the researcher moves back and forth between data collection and analysis, developing and refining along the way). Because changes may be made as part of this process, the reason for these changes needs to be noted and explained.

Autonomy Autonomy is an important ethical principle which requires that potential *participants* have the right and freedom to make their own decision about whether or not they choose to participate in a study.

Axial coding In *qualitative research*, and particularly in *grounded theory*, data are organized into categories (a process called *open coding*) and these categories are then organized again into a theory or model. It is this second stage which is called axial coding.

Bar chart This is a visual way of describing *categorical data*. Each bar in the chart represents a different group within a variable (e.g. blue, brown, and green within the variable 'eye colour') and the height of the bar tells us how many people in each group appear in our data set (in this case, the *frequency distribution*). Because the groups are independent of each other, the bars are always presented with a gap between each one. This type of chart is also called a bar graph. See figure 3.

Bar graph—see *Bar chart*

Bell curve—see *Normal distribution*

Beta coefficient (β) In *regression analysis* the beta coefficient is a number that tells us about the strength of the *relationship* between any given *predictor variable* (*independent variable*) and an

Figure 3 Bar chart

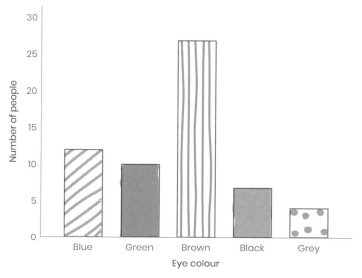

outcome variable (*dependent variable*), expressed in units of *standard deviation*. So it tells us how many standard deviations in the outcome variable are associated with a single standard deviation increase (or decrease) in the predictor variable. This *standardized* beta coefficient is represented by the Greek letter β, but you should be aware that when the coefficient is reported in non-standardized units (i.e. not in standard deviations, but in the original measurements), the letter b is used. Perhaps an example using standardized units would help here? If you were interested in the sort of salary people attract when entering the job market, one factor of interest might be age, and whether or not it affects that salary. Using regression analysis to predict salary (£s per year) based on age, a beta coefficient of 578 for age would mean that for every one-year change in age (i.e. one standard deviation), there is an associated salary increase of £578. (If the beta coefficient was *minus* 578, then for each one-year change in age the salary would *decrease* by £578!)

Between-groups design A between-groups design refers to the way an experimenter has allocated their participants to a condition. As an example, 'type of memory technique', as an *independent variable*, might have two levels (or conditions): a 'rehearsal' level and an 'image-linking' level. The researcher has a choice about how they can test this, and one common choice will be to put half of the participants into the 'rehearsal' level and the other half into the 'image-linking' level, and then compare how they do. This is a between-groups design (otherwise known as an independent-groups design or an unrelated design). See figure 4. You can compare this with other common types of design, e.g. *within-groups design* (otherwise known as a dependent design, related design, or repeated measures design) or the *matched pairs design*.

Between-groups variance Between-groups variance refers to the difference in the spread of scores that you see between groups (or conditions) in an *ANOVA*. If the between-groups

Figure 4 Between-groups design

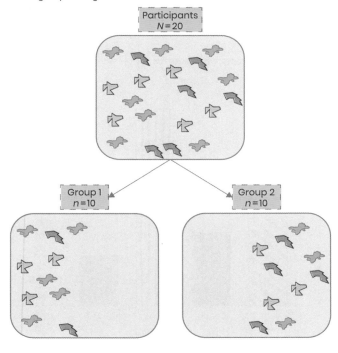

Figure 5 Between-groups variance

$$SS(B) = \sum n(\bar{x} - \bar{x}_{GM})^2 \; \smiley$$

variance is much larger than the *within-groups variance* (or the variance in the participants within a condition) it would suggest that there is likely to be a significant difference between the conditions and that the difference doesn't occur by chance. See figure 5.

Bimodal distribution A bimodal distribution refers to a spread of scores which has two peaks or *modes* (a mode being the most frequently occurring score in a set of scores). The *bar chart* in figure 6 shows a bimodal distribution as it indicates that the most enjoyed card games are equally Gin Rummy and Patience.

Binary logistic regression—see *Logistic regression*

Binary variable A binary variable is a variable that has only two values ('bi' meaning two—think bicycle, bisexual, binary fission. . .). Examples could include 'pass' or 'fail', 'dead' or 'alive', 'yes' or 'no'. Other names for binary variables include *binomial* or *dichotomous* variables.

Binomial variable—see *Binary variable*

Biserial correlation A biserial correlation measures the relationship between two *variables* when one has *continuous* data (*interval* or *ratio*) and the other has artificially produced *binary* data (e.g. a self-esteem scale where participants are divided into high and low groups). Incidentally, the correlation coefficient for a biserial correlation is r_b. See also *Point biserial correlation*.

Bivariate correlation This simply means a *correlation* between two variables, so it is a type of *inferential test* that allows us to understand the relationship between them. If both variables provide *continuous data*, we would use a *Pearson's correlation* whereas if either one (or both) of the variables provide *ordinal data* (or if they fail to meet *parametric assumptions*) we would use a *Spearman's correlation*.

Blind testing This is an experimental procedure used by researchers whereby they don't let their participants know which condition of the study they are taking part in (in other words, participants don't know whether they are in the experimental or the control group). It is used in order to avoid participants affecting (biasing) the results by acting in a way they 'think' they should, rather than how they would naturally. For example, a sports psychologist might want

B

Figure 6 Bimodal distribution

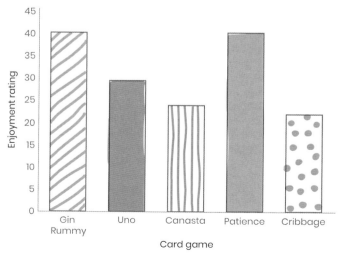

to see if a small amount of caffeine affects task performance. In this case they might give one group a specific measure of caffeine, and the other group a placebo. They would not want participants to try harder (or less hard) just because of the group they are in, so would avoid this situation by not telling them which concoction they have had.

Bonferroni correction This is a method used to adjust the *alpha level* when our data have been used to compare several pairs of groups on multiple occasions. We do it because the more times you test the same data, the more likely you are to find a significant outcome, even if it doesn't really exist (i.e. an increased chance of a *Type I error*, also known here as a *family-wise error*). It involves an adjustment to the standard alpha level, which is worked out by dividing .05 by the number of pairs of analyses to be conducted. For example, a health psychologist might be interested in the weekly chocolate consumption for people aged 20–29, 30–39, and 40–49. If we compared the average difference between the three groups, (i.e. 20–29 vs. 30–39; 20–29 vs. 40–49; 30–39 vs. 40–49) each pair would be tested against the new significance level of $.05/3 = .016$.

Bootstrapping Bootstrapping is a rather wonderful statistical technique that we can use to estimate the value of a *parameter* of a *population* (the parameter being a numerical value that tells us something about the population of interest, with the *mean* of the population being a good example). The problem is that mostly we can't collect the information we need from the whole group, so we have to collect it instead from a representative *sample* of that group and then use that statistic to say something about the population. Bootstrapping is a very clever statistical technique that allows us to calculate a population parameter from a sample by resampling. What does that mean? Well, an example might help. Imagine we want to know how many hours of revision a 'typical' undergraduate student will put in in one day during the week prior to an exam. We ask a sample of five students and they report as follows:

2, 1, 3, 3, 6

In terms of bootstrapping, after recording each of the five students' responses, we can either put this representative sample back into the mix, or we can remove it. If we put it back in, this response may be chosen again, and this allows us to generate a very much larger pool of possible sample means. All of the following would therefore be possible samples generated using bootstrapping:

1, 3, 3, 6, 6

2, 2, 2, 3, 3

1, 6, 2, 3, 1

3, 2, 1, 6, 6

3, 3, 3, 1, 2 etc.

Bootstrapping can generate thousands of variations and so the population mean drawn from these bootstrapped means is akin to having collected thousands of samples without having done all the work! Magic!

Bottom-up reasoning—see *Inductive reasoning*

Boxplot Sometimes referred to as a box-whisker plot (for reasons that will become apparent!), this is a really clever type of graph that provides the reader with all sorts of information about the data for a particular variable. It shows how the data are distributed, includes a *measure of central tendency* (the *median*, actually) and indicates whether there are any *outliers*. Good, eh! The boxplot in Figure 7 shows the data for a study which was interested in how well older people can concentrate on the world around them. Levels of concentration were specifically measured in terms of different tasks and conversations. The boxplots allow us to compare the distribution of the data for these two variables. The box itself (the coloured bit) represents the middle 50% of all the values in the distribution. It is known as the *interquartile range*. The line across each box represents the median value for each task (a measure of central tendency). The 'whiskers'—the lines sticking out of each end of the box—represent up to 25% of the data above the middle section and 25% of the data below the middle section (but do not include data that are more than 1 box length away from the ends of the box—those data are *outliers*). The circles and asterisks represent outliers.

Figure 7 Boxplot

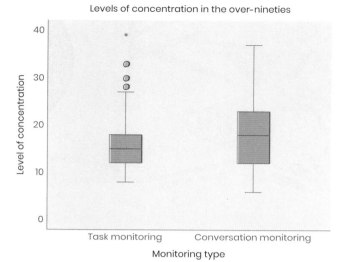

Levels of concentration in the over-nineties

If the data point is more than 1 box length but less than 1.5 box lengths away from the end of the box (above or below), it is indicated with a circle 'o'. If it is more than 1.5 box lengths away from the end of the box, this is an extreme outlier, and is indicated with an asterisk '*'. The two boxplots in this example suggest that the spread of scores (*variability*) is bigger for conversation monitoring than for task monitoring, but the median score for task monitoring is lower than for conversation monitoring (although the highest overall score was for task monitoring—the extreme outlier).

Box's test When we conduct more complex analyses such as a *MANOVA* where there is more than one *dependent variable*, we need to be sure that the variance (or spread of scores) between all of the dependent variables is similar—like *homogeneity of variance* in a test with just one dependent variable. Box's test (or Box's M test) is what we use to check this. Just like other tests of homogeneity, we are looking for a non-significant outcome (because we don't want the spread of scores in our groups to be significantly different from each other). However, because this test is very sensitive (aren't we all sometimes!), and gets more so as the number of DV's increases, we use a smaller *alpha* level than normal when

we interpret it, so for the Box's test, the p value needs to be greater than .001 ($p > .001$) for us to be happy that the variance is similar.

Box-whisker plot—see *Boxplot*

Bracketing In some *qualitative research*, especially *phenomenology*, but also other approaches where interviews or observations are used, bracketing is an important process which reflects the stance of the researcher. By bracketing, the researcher sets aside any personal experiences, ideas, or biases about the topic under investigation in order to be as objective as possible. In effect, they are putting their own preconceptions to one side so that research topic remains at the centre of the study. The process itself lacks consensus between researchers, but if you want to read more, see Tufford and Newman (2010).

Tufford, L. & Newman, P. (2010). Bracketing in qualitative research. *Qualitative Social Work*, *11*(1), 80–96. Doi:10.1177/1473325010368316

Brown-Forsythe *F* In a *one-way ANOVA*, when the assumption of *homogeneity of variance* has not been met, Brown-Forsythe *F* provides an alternative statistic to the *F*-ratio. *Welch's F* is, however, a similar test to Brown-Forsythe *F* and tends to be the option of choice.

Case study Used primarily in qualitative research, a case study is a detailed or in-depth investigation. This would usually be of an individual but could also be of a group of individuals (for example, a particular social group, a work organization, a University class, or a community), or an event or situation that is being studied or individuals who are under some form of treatment. In other words, a case study is not a choice about method, but instead a choice about what is to be studied.

Categorical data—see *Nominal data*

Categorical design A categorical design is simply a design which uses *nominal* or *categorical variables*

Categorical variable A categorical variable is any variable that uses data which are grouped by a particular category, and which allows us to count how many participants/bits of data belong in each one (*nominal data*), as opposed to measuring it (*interval* or *ratio data*) or noting its position within some sort of ranking (*ordinal data*). For example, socio-economic status and degree classification are both categorical variables, as each person could only belong in one group.

Causal hypothesis—see *Experimental hypothesis*

Ceiling effect This describes what happens when a measure is not sensitive enough to

capture a range of scores, and the majority of scores recorded are clustered at the higher end of the scale being used, or are the maximum score. For example, if your lecturer wants to see whether a new teaching method improves your knowledge, and your class scored near 100% on a test prior to any intervention, then it would be hard for scores to increase and it would not allow for any improvements to be detected. See how this compares to a '*floor effect*'.

Cells A cell is the space in a table created where a row crosses a column. In *ANOVA*, every cell will represent a group. For example, in Table 1, the cell representing the bisection of the row 'students' with the column 'signed up' shows the frequency count for students who have signed up for a salsa class (in this case 64 students have signed up—nice!).

Central Limit Theorem This is a really important concept in statistics (and maths, too, actually) and starts with an understanding of *sampling distribution*. (If you're not clear about this it would be a good idea to read up on it first). Essentially it says that if we have a large enough *sample* (and we can start to relax at around 30 or more), then our sampling distribution will start to take on the shape of the aptly named 'bell curve' or '*normal distribution*'. What's more, that will be true *even if* the population that you've taken your sample from isn't normally distributed. Why is that so important?

Table 1 Cells

	Signed up	Not signed up	Total
Teachers	45	135	180
Students	64	214	278
Total	109	349	458

Well—because the normal distribution allows statisticians to analyse a whole load of statistical problems, which then lets us generalize from samples to populations. And *that's* important!

Central tendency—see *Measure of central tendency*

Chi Square (χ^2) Note: this is not pronounced 'Chi' as in 'China', but 'Ki' as in 'Kite'! Although Chi Square (χ^2) can refer to a number of statistical tests, it generally refers to what is, named in full, Pearson's Chi Squared Test. It is an *inferential test* that is used when we want to investigate whether there is a statistically significant association between two *categorical variables*. It does this by comparing the differences between *observed frequencies* (what we actually see) and *expected frequencies* (theoretically, what we might expect to see given the *null hypothesis*). The larger the difference between observed and expected frequencies, the more likely it is that the association did not occur by chance (i.e. that it is significant).

Closed questions When we conduct an *interview* or a *survey*, closed questions are those that are answered with a simple *'Yes'* or *'No'*, or which have a specific response format. An example might be: *'Did you enjoy your trip?'* to which the choice of answers might be a) yes, a lot; b) yes, a little; c) no, not very much; d) no, it was awful! This could be compared to the *open-ended question 'What can you tell me about your trip?'*. So in a closed question the person answering doesn't have the opportunity to expand on what they want to say. Closed questions are often used in surveys to get a lot of responses which are easily analysed.

Cluster Analysis Cluster Analysis is an overarching term for a number of exploratory methods used in various *multivariate* analyses (e.g. *MANOVA, Discriminant analysis,* etc.) which aim to separate data into groups based on similar characteristics (and if you know anything about computing and data mining, you're in safe water here!). Having conducted a cluster analysis, the groups you have formed should share similarities in *variables* within the cluster and they should be distinct from the same variables in another cluster. For example, in terms of the variable 'extraversion', one cluster

Figure 8 Cluster analysis

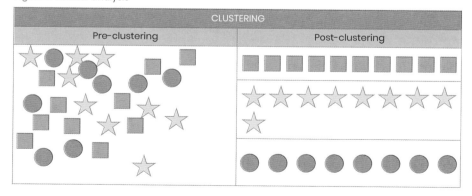

C

of participants may all identify as extraverts, whereas in another cluster participants may identify as introverts. As an exploratory method it is *descriptive* by nature but can then be used in inferential analyses to look for differences between the formulated groups. See figure 8.

Clustered sampling This is a *sampling* approach which divides the population of interest into groups or clusters. It is used when the groups are, in themselves, pretty similar, but the individuals within them are quite diverse. There are usually two stages. The first stage would be to divide your *population* into similar groups. You would then pick an appropriate number of groups from the total to work with, perhaps by *random* or *systematic sampling*. The second stage would be to pick individuals from within those groups, again, using an appropriate sampling method. (You could, however, use all participants in each of your selected groups, in which case this would be 'one-stage cluster sampling').

An example, here, might help. Imagine a researcher wants to understand the exercise habits of children in secondary education in the UK. Rather than trying to interview them all, in the first stage they might divide the UK into regions of equal population size (groups) and then choose three groups, one from the North, one from the Midlands, and one from the South. In the second stage, they might then interview every tenth child from a list of all children within each particular group. See also *Stratified sampling* for a comparison.

Clustering—see *Cluster analysis*

Coding When we use the term 'coding' we may mean different things, depending on whether we are a *qualitative* or *quantitative* researcher. As a qualitative researcher, coding is an analytical process in which you work through a transcript and make notes, generally in the margin alongside the original data, on the perceived meaning of sentences or segments of the data. These notes are then used to identify overarching concepts. It is the first part of the process in analysing and understanding your data after having transcribed them. As a quantitative researcher, coding means something different. Here, when you 'code' data you are changing a *categorical* variable (i.e. a

variable with *nominal* level data) into a numerical variable in preparation for a numerical analysis. For example, if you want to analyse age differences in spatial rotation tasks, age (young/old) is a categorical variable but needs to be analysed numerically, so you could code 'young' as '1' and 'old' as '2' (or, indeed, the other way round as the code is simply a numerical identifier).

Coefficient of correlation—see *Correlation coefficient*

Coefficient of determination—see R^2

Coefficient of multiple determination—see R^2

Cohen's d Cohen's *d* is a measure of *effect size* (or how large the effect of something is) used to quantify the difference between two groups (see Table C, Effect sizes). Essentially, a *d* of 1 says that two groups differ by one standard deviation, a *d* of 2 by two standard deviations and so on. If that has switched you right off, though, you can use the 'rule of thumb' guidelines offered by Cohen (1988), i.e.:

• Larger than – 0.2 Small effect

• Larger than – 0.5 Medium effect

• Larger than – 0.8 Large effect.

So, for example, if you have a *d* of 1.3, you have a large effect size representing 1.3 standard deviations between the groups. A practical footnote: if you are considering reporting Cohen's *d* as your effect size and have a sample of more than 50, go ahead. If, however, your sample is smaller, consider instead using Hedge's *g* as Cohen's *d* can rather over-inflate results.

Cohen, J. (1988). *Statistical power analysis for the behavioral sciences* (2nd ed.). New York: Academic Press.

Cohort effect A cohort is a group of people who share something in common. This is often having been born in a particular period of time (and therefore having been exposed to the same socio-cultural and political influences as each other), but it could also be through having shared a common life experience around the same time. These shared experiences may shape their perspectives in a way which we call the 'cohort effect'. For example, being a teenager in post-war Britain would shape attitudes towards life which could be quite different to millennials, or, indeed, those of a pre-war cohort.

Collinearity—see *Multicollinearity*

Competence Competence, as a guiding ethical principle, is the requirement that psychologists recognize the limits to their own expertise (or competence) and practise within those limits, whether that is with regard to their research, their teaching, or in their practice.

Component matrix In principal components analysis, a form of *factor analysis*, this is the general term used to describe the table of *correlations* between the items and the components that is produced when you conduct the analysis. See also *Structure matrix*.

Concurrent validity This form of validity considers how well the score on one measure relates to (or agrees with) those obtained from one or more other measures all assessed *at the same time*. For example, if you wanted to see if your new test of short-term memory was a valid measure, you would correlate/compare your participants' scores on your test with their scores on an established measure of short-term memory, both completed at the same time. A strong correlation between the two sets of scores would indicate that the two are measuring the same thing, therefore your new measure could be considered a valid way to assess short-term memory. It is a type of *criterion validity*.

Condition When a researcher is carrying out *experimental* research they want to manipulate the *independent variable* or conditions (groups) in it, to see if that has an effect on the *dependent variable*. For example, they might want to see whether the introduction of a daily yoga class at an old people's home improves their physical well-being. So, they might introduce such a yoga class in one old people's home, but not in a similar home. The first is the *experimental condition*, the second the *control condition*. The condition may be a *categorical variable*. For example, a study on age differences would probably have two groups for age, (young and old), or an amount (e.g. a study on therapeutic levels of a drug might look at Condition A, 5mg of the drug, Condition B, 10mg and so on) or even a time point (e.g. a study looking at a teaching intervention may compare exam scores at week 0, week 6, and week 12, representing Conditions 1, 2, and 3 respectively).

Confidence interval When we conduct research we often use a sample, but we want to be sure that a parameter—generally the *mean* value we present—is truly representative of the whole population. One way to do this is by calculating boundaries (upper and lower) for a range of values that we believe will contain the true population mean. These boundaries are called Confidence Intervals, and are generally set at 95% (most often used) or 99% (sometimes used) to give us confidence that 95% or 99% of the time the population mean will fall within them. So the aim here is to allow us to generalize the data to a whole population.

Confidentiality Confidentiality is one of the ethical principles we need to consider when conducting research, and it relates to the protection of the data that are collected. The researcher should be able to identify individual participants and link them to their data, but this information must not be shared with anyone, so data are stored carefully, using unique identifying labels.

Confirmatory factor analysis—see *Factor analysis*

Confounding variable When researchers design an experiment we want to be sure that we can infer cause and effect. In other words, if we manipulate one variable (the *independent variable* or *IV*), we want to know that any change noted in the *dependent variable* (the *DV* or outcome variable) is as a result of the manipulation we made. Sometimes that might not be the case and the outcome might be better explained by the influence of another variable we had not taken into account in our experimental design, known as a confounding variable. A confounding variable, of course, then makes it impossible to infer causation. An example? If we want to test gender differences in memory of emotion-laden words, we might test female students for emotion-laden words in our morning seminar and male students for the same words in our afternoon seminar. The results initially show the male students with a higher mean score. The problem is, students (female or otherwise), often don't like mornings much (and who can blame them?), and so the female students may not be as engaged with the task as the now-perky males. So, it may be that time of day better explains the higher mean score in the male students for emotion-laden words than gender. Time of day becomes, then, a confounding variable.

Consent Potential research participants need to be given sufficient information about a research project so that they can decide whether to take part or not. If they do choose to take part, they are giving their consent. Sometimes, however, it is important to withhold some information (incomplete disclosure) so that participants remain naïve to the study and do not alter their behaviour to please (or upset!) the researcher. It is okay to do this (it is not the same as *deception*), but the research then needs to ensure that a full account of the research project is given at the end of the study (*debrief*). Please have a look at *Informed consent* for a slightly different approach.

Constructionism—see *Constructivism*

Constructivism This is a research philosophy that argues that *any individual's understanding* of the nature of being or reality is socially constructed and subjective and is therefore open to interpretation (and hence its other name—interpretivism). Constructivists *may* accept that there is an 'outside reality' (or they may not!), but they would argue that how it is recognized and understood could, and probably will, differ from one individual to the next (in contrast to a positivist approach which argues that reality is 'out there' whether we have any conscious awareness of it or not). Because it is about the nature of being, it is an *ontological* position. An example could be 'gender'. A constructivist position would argue that what is regarded as 'gender' is an individual's construction or product of the time and place we live in—it may or may not have a real 'essence' of its own. In addition to *constructivism and interpretivism*, it is also known as constructionism.

Construct validity Simply put, a measurement technique (or tool) has construct validity if the measure accurately reflects the concepts and construct that interests us. As an example,

'sociosexuality' (the disposition to engage in sexual activity outside of a committed relationship) is made up of three areas, 'sociosexual desire', 'sociosexual attitude', and 'sociosexual behaviour'. If you only asked participants questions about their sociosexual behaviour, you would not be capturing the whole construct. This element of construct validity is known as *content* validity. In addition, to have construct validity a measure should have both *convergent validity* (if a measure really works we would expect it to relate to other measures that test similar things) and *discriminant validity* (if a measure really works we would *not* expect it to relate to measures of other variables that we understand to be theoretically distinct). See Figure 46 for a list of other kinds of validity.

Content analysis This is a fairly general term which refers to several techniques used by researchers to transform *qualitative data* into *quantitative data*. Quite often content analyses will involve media, i.e. newspapers, television, films, the internet, etc. The researcher will use content analysis to find *coding* categories that describe substantial aspects of the data, and then quantify how often those categories occur. For example, content analysis was used by the US Government to investigate the use of propaganda during WW2.

Content validity Content validity is a component of *construct validity* and is concerned with how well your test really measures the construct you are interested in. For example, if you wanted to measure someone's ability to do maths, and you only asked them how to do long division, your test would not be valid because it would not represent all aspects of maths ability. We would use experts to help ensure that all relevant aspects of a topic are included. See Figure 46 for a list of other kinds of validity.

Contingency table A contingency table is a table that shows the *frequency counts* of two or more *categorical variables* and is therefore a useful table to offer when using *Chi Square* as the statistical analysis. The contingency table may also include column and row percentages, making comparison between variables more

Table 2 Contingency table

	Completed a Research Methods module		
	Yes	No	Total
Fear of Statistics	22	105	127
No	29	108	137
Total	51	213	264

meaningful. For example, Table 2 indicates fear of statistics (Yes/No) for students who have or have not completed a Research Methods module (though why there are 22 students who have a fear of stats once they had completed their Research Methods module we are at a loss to understand!)

Continuous data Continuous data is the name that is given to two *levels of measurement* (or means of measuring data): *interval data* (continuous data with no real zero) and *ratio data* (continuous data but with a real zero). The consistent factor here is that we are talking about data that have been measured on a continuum of equal intervals. So height, exam scores, time, salary, even the cost of a burger, are continuous variables as each unit of measurement for any given variable is the same (i.e. height is measured in centimetres, exam scores in marks out of 100, time in seconds, and so on). They are often grouped together because analyses tend not to distinguish between the two.

Contrast analyses These are a specific set of statistical procedures which allow us to compare the *pattern* (rather than the *significance*) of differences between two or more groups of *data*. They are generally used when we want to address a specific *research question* about those differences, or in other words, when we are considering an a priori comparison. Have a look at *helmert contrast* and *polynomial contrast* for two examples.

Control group/condition A control group is a group of participants used as a benchmark for comparison with an *experimental group*. Impor-

tantly, unlike the experimental group who are exposed to some sort of procedure or treatment by the researcher, the control group does not receive any such intervention.

Controlled observation In a controlled observation the researcher observes behaviour under, as the name suggests, controlled conditions! It is still an observation, so the researcher will observe behaviour or events and record what happens, but the environment in which this happens has been organized to allow the research question to be addressed. A seminal example of a controlled observation would be Bandura's (1961) Bobo doll study.

Bandura, A., Ross, D. & Ross, S.A. (1961). Transmission of aggression through imitation of aggressive models. *Journal of Abnormal and Social Psychology, 63*, 575–82.

Convergent validity If a measure really works we would expect it to relate to other measures that test the same or related things; this is known as convergent validity. For example, if we were trying to assess people's happiness, we would expect scores on the Satisfaction with Life Scale (Deiner, Emmons, Larson & Griffin, 1985) to relate to scores on the Subjective Happiness Scale (Lyubomirsky & Leper, 1999). Convergent validity is one of the ways that we assess the '*construct validity*' of a measure (and is the opposite of *discriminant validity*).

Convenience sampling—see *Opportunity sampling* (see Table E on page 108)

Conversation analysis The way we speak to our friends at a party is likely to be very different to the way we communicate with our doctor or the police. In order to understand how we navigate these different kinds of social interactions, researchers use conversation analysis (often abbreviated to CA), which is a very detailed study of the methods (both words and nonverbal communications) we use in different situations in everyday life. For example, researchers using CA might be interested not only in what specific words used during a conversation tell us, but also what the pauses between words and increased volume applied to different words convey. Overall this approach provides a very detailed understanding of all aspects of an interaction between people.

Cook's distance (Cook's *D*) Used in *regression analysis*, Cook's distance is a measure that helps us to identify *outliers* in our *predictor variables*. It is important to check this because a single outlier can have a strong influence on the overall analysis, and might affect the *validity* of our findings and our interpretation of the results. As a rule of thumb, if we get a Cook's *D* value that is greater than 1 it will be cause for concern.

Correlation A correlation is a measure of how closely two *variables* relate to each other, so it is simply the *relationship* between two variables. It is usually reported as a single number, a *correlation coefficient*, which tells us the strength and direction of the relationship. When reporting this the correlation coefficient is usually denoted by the letter *r*.

Correlation coefficient A correlation coefficient is a number between −1 and +1 which expresses both the strength and direction of a statistical relationship between two or more variables. If the number is close to 0 it is likely that

there is no linear relationship. If, on the other hand, the number is close to −1 or +1, then the relationship exists, and the closer it is to −1 or +1 the stronger the relationship is. The negative or positive sign tells you about the direction of the relationship. If the sign is positive (+), this means that as the scores on one variable increase, so, too, do the scores on the other. If the sign is negative (−), this means that as the scores on one variable increase, the scores on the other variable decrease. See figure 9.

R is used when reporting multiple correlations, whereas *r* is used when reporting bivariate correlations (see also *Correlation, Positive Correlation,* and *Negative correlation* for more information).

Correlational research This is a type of research which looks at the relationship between two or more variables. Importantly, unlike *experimental research*, we cannot determine cause and effect from a correlational design because the researcher does not manipulate the variables, but we can investigate how variables might work together and how they are related to each other.

Counterbalancing When researchers use a *within-groups design* there can be a problem with *order effects*. To solve this problem the different conditions of the study need to be presented to participants in all possible orders. This is known as counterbalancing. So, if a researcher wanted to study the effect of different memory techniques on later recall of information—e.g. a) image linking, b) rehearsal, and c) mnemonics—they would ask some participants to do image linking first, followed by rehearsal, and then mnemonics; and some participants to do rehearsal first, followed by

Figure 9 Correlation coefficient

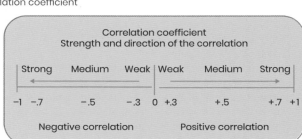

mnemonics, followed by image linking; and so on. So the starting condition and order of completing the other conditions will differ for participants. In this case there would be six different orders to consider, e.g. ABC, BCA, CAB etc! You might also want to look at *Latin square*, *order effects*, and *practice effects*.

Covariance This is a measure of how much the changes in one *variable* are related to changes in another variable, and it can be calculated for many different statistics, e.g. *ANCOVA, MANOVA, regression*, etc. For example, a developmental researcher may be interested in the link between parents reading to children and early progress of a child's own reading skills. Positive covariance would be found if an increase in the time spent reading to children was related to an improvement in children's reading ability. If you love statistics, you might like to know that while both correlations and covariance are measures of the linear relationship between two variables, covariance, unlike correlation, does not use standardized units to measure the linear relationship between them!

Co-variable—see *Covariate*

Covariate A covariate is a *predictor variable* that has some relationship with the *outcome variable* we are interested in. Typically we want to 'control for' or remove the effect of the covariate to see the remaining influence of the other predictor variable(s) on the outcome variable. For example, a researcher is interested in the possible relationship between time spent on Instagram and subjective wellbeing. However, they feel that 'social comparison' may also have an influence on that relationship and therefore will want to control for the effect of that variable too. So, the covariate, here, is 'social comparison'. The covariate is different from a confounding variable in that it is accounted for in the original research design.

Covert observation In a covert observation those who are being observed are *not* made aware of the fact by the researcher. There are two types—*non-participant* and *participant*. With covert non-participant observation the researcher has no direct contact with the people being observed and they are not aware they are being studied. In covert participant observation the researcher infiltrates the group by pretending to be an ordinary member of it. You can see that although they both have the potential to provide some really interesting data, they are fraught with ethical issues! How would you feel if you found your group had been infiltrated by someone who was simply recording and analysing the things you did within that group?!

Cramer's V This is a measure of *effect size* (see Table C, Effect sizes). Specifically it is a test of the strength of the association between two categorical variables, used when conducting a *Chi Square*. Importantly, it is used when one or both of the variables has more than two categories (e.g. a 2×3 design or a 3×4 design). It is measured between 0 (no association between the variables) and 1 (absolute association), where (according to Cohen, 1988) a small effect size would be between .1 and .3, a medium effect size would be between .3 and .5 and a large effect size would be greater than .5. You may want to look at Chi Square for more information about the background to this. See also *Phi correlation*.

Cohen, J. (1988). *Statistical power and analysis for the behavioral sciences.* (2nd ed.), Hillsdale, N.J., Lawrence Erlbaum Associates, Inc.

Criterion validity Criterion validity is a method for assessing whether a test really measures what it intends to measure (i.e. has *validity*) by comparing it with another measure, see figure 10. It is an umbrella term for two types of validity. If the two measures are taken at the same time (for example, a longer version and an abbreviated version of a Happiness Questionnaire) we are measuring a particular kind of criterion validity called *concurrent validity*. If, on the other hand, the two measures are taken at different times, the particular kind of criterion validity we are looking at is called *predictive validity*. For either to be valid (concurrent or predictive) scores would need to be similar for both.

Criterion variable This is another name for the *dependent variable*, and is used alongside the *predictor variable(s)*. It is also called the outcome variable and this is the term most often used in non-experimental studies. For example, a lecturer wants to know whether

Figure 10 Criterion validity

Oxford Happiness Inventory (original)

89%

Oxford Happiness Questionnaire (revised)

86%

intelligence and the time spent revising (both predictor variables) can be used to predict the scores that have been obtained in a recent test (criterion variable).

Critical value Critical values are used in *hypothesis* testing. The critical value is the point on a *normal distribution curve* that separates the 'reject' region (indicating when you can reject the *null hypothesis*) from the 'accept' region (in other words, that lovely moment when you find you have a *significant* result). It is dependent on the chosen *alpha level* and the type of statistical test being conducted, and there may be one, or more than one, critical value depending on whether you are testing a *one* or *two-tailed hypothesis*. If you were to carry out your analysis by hand (???) you would need to find

the relevant critical value (found in tables in the back of all good stats textbooks) and compare this with your *observed value* in order to assess significance. See table 3.

Cronbach's alpha When we create a questionnaire it consists of a number of different questions that all relate to a single concept (actually, they are better termed 'items' as they are not always in the form of a question). Cronbach's alpha is the measure we use to see how reliably/consistently all of these items work together (i.e. the *internal reliability*, or are they really all measuring the same concept?) and is a score that ranges from 0 to 1, with scores at the higher end of the range (above .7) indicating that the items *are* all measuring the same thing. For example, if we want to investigate how happy people are at work, we might ask them to indicate how much they agree/disagree with a number of items, such as '*The amount of work I'm asked to do is appropriate*' or '*I get along well with my colleagues*'. Items like these should all produce a reasonably high Cronbach's alpha, but imagine, now, that the item '*I enjoy my sport*' was added to the questionnaire. This presumably would not work well with the other items and would therefore be likely to reduce the Cronbach's alpha score. One more point: sometimes questionnaires are comprised of a number of subscales, in which case Cronbach's alpha could also be used to measure how well the items in each individual subscale work together.

Cross-sectional research Cross-sectional research can be seen as an 'observational snapshot in time' which allows researchers to look at a particular issue with information coming from diverse groups of people. For example, a researcher might be interested in the impact of social media on body esteem. They might choose to measure the body esteem of two groups, those who use social media all of the time and those who think 'Twitter' is the (surprisingly popular) site for ornithologists online. They might also add another layer—perhaps the under-30s and the over 30s. What they wouldn't do would be to look at these groups over time, as this would then become a *longitudinal study*.

Cubic trend A lot of the analyses we conduct in psychology assume that the data will form

Table 3 Critical value for t tests

df	Level of Signficance - One-Tailed Test				
	0.100	0.050	0.025	0.010	0.001
	Level of Signficance - Two-Tailed Test				
	0.200	0.100	0.050	0.020	0.002
20	1.325	1.725	2.086	2.528	2.845
21	1.323	1.721	2.080	2.518	2.831
22	1.321	1.717	2.074	2.508	2.819
23	1.319	1.714	2.069	2.500	2.807
24	1.318	1.711	2.064	2.492	2.797
25	1.316	1.708	2.060	2.485	2.787
26	1.315	1.706	2.056	2.479	2.779
27	1.314	1.703	2.052	2.473	2.771
28	1.313	1.701	2.048	2.467	2.763
29	1.311	1.699	2.045	2.462	2.756
30	1.310	1.697	2.042	2.457	2.750
40	1.303	1.684	2.021	2.423	2.704
60	1.296	1.671	2.000	2.390	2.660
120	1.289	1.658	1.980	2.358	2.617

C

a linear pattern—a straight line when plotted on a graph. But not all data follow this pattern. When the data have two changes in direction, either upwards or downwards, it is called a cubic trend. Compare this with a *linear trend*, *quadratic trend*, and *quartic trend*. See also *Trend analysis* and Figure 44.

Cumulative frequency distribution A cumulative *frequency distribution* takes a tally of the number of scores in each group across a set of groups and then provides a running total. When might that be useful? Imagine we are throwing a party for 50 people and we want to please at least 60% of them with their favourite pudding, i.e. 30 of the 50 party-go-ers. We can see from Table 4 that we only need to take three options (Eton Mess, Sticky Toffee Pudding, and Banoffee Pie) to do so, as they represent 33 of the 50 people.

Table 4 Cumulative frequency distribution

Pudding preference	Frequency	Cumulative total
Eton Mess	13	13
Sticky Toffee Pudding	15	28
Banoffee Pie	5	33
Cheesecake	8	41
Apple Pie and Custard	6	47
Other	3	50
Total	50	

Data Any information collected by a research-er is called data. Although you are probably thinking that data are always 'numbers', so quantitative, this is not the case. Interview transcripts, videos, drawings, etc. more asso-ciated with qualitative research are also data. Remember that 'data' is plural, and the singular is 'datum'!

Debrief This is an important ethical process which occurs at the end of the participation pe-riod, and is when the researcher clearly explains the purpose of the study to anyone taking part. It is particularly important when anything other than fully *informed consent* has been obtained. It is also an opportunity to offer the participants answers to any questions they may have about the study, and, in addition, to provide links to appropriate support agencies. (Remember that even the most innocuous study might evoke some negative psychological response, either immediately or at some future point—we never know!)

Deception Deception is when participants taking part in a piece of research are delib-erately misinformed about the nature of the research, i.e. they are told that it is about one thing when really it is concerned with some-thing entirely different. Ethically this needs serious consideration. An extreme example of this is the 'Electric shock' study conducted by

Stanley Milgram in the 1960s. He recruited participants on the understanding that he was interested in memory and learning, when he was really looking at obedience to authority! A better way to conduct research, if naivety is required, is to withhold information until the debrief (this is *not* deception), at which point full information about the nature of the study is offered, and consent obtained again if needed.

Milgram, S. (1963). Behavioral study of obedience. *Journal of Abnormal and Social Psychology, 67*, 371–8.

Deductive method The (hypothetico-) deductive method is a particular approach to the way we conduct research using hypothesis test-ing to reach its conclusions. It starts with a clear, testable hypothesis that is deduced or inferred from theory. That hypothesis is then tested and the results analysed to see whether the hypothe-sis may or may not be supported. You can think of it as a 'top-down' approach as it moves from the abstract to the specific, in contrast to the *inductive method* which moves from the specific to a more abstract level.

Deductive reasoning Also known as logical reasoning, and therefore, (logically!) it is reason-ing based on a set of statements that lead us to a logical conclusion. An example could be:

All humans are in the genus *Homo*. Gertrude is a human. Gertrude is in the genus *Homo*.

A *hypothesis* may be arrived at through this form of reasoning, and will then be tested empirically through data collection for its 'truth'. Deductive reasoning is also called top-down reasoning and can be compared to *inductive reasoning* or bottom-up reasoning.

Degrees of freedom You usually see this reported as '*df*', and it is an important number that helps us to interpret the outcome of many of the inferential tests we conduct, e.g. *Chi Square*, *t-test* or *F-ratio*. When we are calculating the test statistic it tells us how many of the values in our data set are independent and free to vary (. . .WHAT?)

OK, imagine you've just had a birthday party and four of your friends couldn't make it. Because you are a kind person, you want to give each of them one of the cupcakes you made for the occasion (not only kind, but a good baker, too!). So, when you see the first friend, they have the choice of all four cupcakes (see figure 11). The second friend then chooses their favourite from the three that are left, and that leaves two friends and two cupcakes. One of those remaining friends will still have a choice from the two that are left, but the fourth friend will have to have whichever cupcake is left. In this example there are three degrees of freedom, three independent choices that could vary, before the fate of the final cupcake is decided.

Importantly, in order to be able to conduct our inferential analyses and generalize our findings from our sample to the population of interest, we need to know the number of degrees of freedom since this information is an integral part of many equations. We can demonstrate that most easily in relation to Chi Square. The *df* for this analysis is worked out by multiplying the number of rows minus 1 ($R - 1$) by the number of columns minus 1 ($C - 1$). So, the more categories there are in each variable, the more *df*'s there are. In a study where you are interested in colour preference between children and adults, if the choice is between 'yellow' and 'blue', then we have a 2 × 2 design—two categories for 'lifespan stage' and two categories for 'colour'. To work out the *df* we would calculate $(R - 1)(C - 1)$, which is $(2 - 1)(2 - 1)$, which $= 1 \times 1$, which $= 1$! Now, if we add some more colours into the study (red and green), we will have created a 2 × 4 design. The *df* is now $(2 - 1)(4 - 1)$, which $= 1 \times 3$, which $= 3$.

Demand characteristics Demand characteristics are any aspects of a psychological study which, consciously or otherwise, exert some pressure on the participants to behave or respond in a particular way. For example, Orme and Scheibe (1964) investigated demand characteristics through a sensory deprivation study. All participants were asked to sit in a small, comfy room for four hours (no texting— no internet . . . Really?). Participants in the *experimental condition* were told it was a sensory deprivation study and were required to fill in a release form and given a panic button to press if they became stressed. Participants in the control group were not given these instructions or equipment. Low and behold, no stress was seen in the control participants, but it was in the experimental group!

Orme, M.T. & Scheibe, K.E. (1964). The contribution of non-deprivation factors in the production of sensory deprivation effects: The psychology of the panic button. *Journal of Abnormal and Social Psychology*, 68(1), 3–12.

Figure 11 Degrees of freedom

Dependent design—see *Within-groups design*

Dependent *t*-test—see *Paired samples t-test*

Dependent variable (DV) The clue is in the name as the dependent variable *depends* on the manipulation of another variable of interest to the researcher. In research we often want to test whether, by manipulating one thing (the *independent variable*), it affects another thing (the dependent variable). As an example, imagine that a developmental psychologist wants to see whether pre-school literacy affects the confidence of schoolchildren in their first year at infant school. In this case, the independent variable would be literacy and the dependent variable would be confidence. They could divide pre-school children into groups (the independent variable of literacy being broken down into low/moderate and high conditions) and see how those groups compare at the end of the first year in confidence levels (the dependent variable).

Descriptive statistics Descriptive statistics are so named because, in one way or another, they describe or summarize our data. This could be by offering averages (e.g. *means, medians,* or *modes*), or *measures of dispersion* (perhaps the *range* or *standard deviation*). It could also be through graphical representation of the data (perhaps through *bar graphs* or *scatterplots*). We can compare descriptive statistics with *inferential statistics* which are used, instead, to make inferences (draw conclusions) about a *population* from a *sample* drawn from that population.

Design (lab report) The design, importantly, describes the framework or outline of the research, and is reported within the *Method section* of your research report. You should state, for example, whether the research was *experimental* or not. If it was, you would need to explain how participants were allocated to the *condition*s of the study and whether there was any *control group*. You would also need to report whether a *between* or *within-groups design* was used, what the *independent* and *dependent variable(s)* were, etc. If not experimental, you would include comments on the approach used (e.g. an *observational* design), and you would include sufficient description of the research in order to allow the reader to understand how the study was conducted and could be repeated in the same way in the future if desired.

df—see *Degrees of freedom*

Diary method This is a method of data collection that requires participants to keep a daily record of activities and/or experiences that are of interest to the researcher. It is a very useful method when you want to collect regular information over a period of time or are concerned that the presence of a researcher might influence people's responses. The diary (which might also be called a journal or a log), can be very structured—e.g. participants could be asked to record how they feel about themselves at regular intervals (once a day, every morning, afternoon and evening, at mealtimes, etc.), or much more unstructured—participants could be asked to record any thoughts on the first few weeks of a new job.

Dichotomous variable A dichotomous variable is a special kind of *categorical variable* (or anything that is measured by the number of data within a category). It is special because there are only two categories (or levels) of the variable. For example, 'dead' or 'alive' would be a rather basic but clear outcome variable which would be dichotomous, as would 'pass' or 'fail', or 'student' or 'teacher'.

Directional hypothesis—see *One-tailed hypothesis*

Direct oblimin When conducting *factor analysis* this is a method of *oblique rotation* that is commonly used. It lets us identify underlying *factors* in the data when all the variables are correlated with each other. If you want more information about this, do have a look at the entry for oblique rotation to cast more light on the matter!

Discourse analysis Discourse analysis centres on the detailed study of patterns used in the language and the meaning drawn from them. This may be within naturally occurring interactions, interviews, or group discussions, and may be produced specifically for research or not. Importantly it is a constructivist approach, in which language does not just reflect meaning, but actually creates it. Think about it like this: in our amazing language we have lots of different words that mean more or less the same thing (e.g. claim, demand, or appeal for) and the ones we choose to use build the picture we want to paint, whether conscious or not. Now consider the difference between, 'Model makes an appeal for £100,000 in compensation' and 'Model cashes in with demand for £100,000 in compensation'. Has your impression of the model been influenced by the language used?

Discrete variable—see *Categorical variable*

Discriminant (Function) Analysis
Discriminant analysis is a kind of analysis that allows a researcher to categorize two or more *continuous variables* into specified groups. So it's a form of *regression analysis*, but with discriminant analysis the *dependent* variable is *categorical*, not continuous. An example should help. A financial analyst might want to know what factors might be likely to place individuals into a debt situation. The dependent variable might therefore be 'in debt' or 'not in debt' and this information would be known at the start. The purpose of the analysis would be to see how well we can predict which group an individual would be placed in, 'debt' or 'no debt', based on the predictor variables like income, age, family size, attitude towards debt, and so on. It is also sometimes called discriminant function analysis, and if there are more than two categories (debt/no debt/was once in debt), it is called multiple discriminant analysis. You can compare this with *logistic regression*, but whereas discriminant analysis is really only interested in categorization, logistic regression is more interested in the possible relationship between the *predictor variable(s)* and a *categorical outcome variable*.

Discriminant validity If a measure really works we would *not* expect it to relate to certain other variables that we understand to be theoretically distinct from the variable of interest. This is known as discriminant validity. For example, if we were trying to assess people's body esteem, we would *not* expect scores on the Body Esteem Scale (Franzoi & Shields, 1984) to relate to scores on a scale measuring procrastination (e.g. Lay, 1986). Discriminant validity is one

of the ways that we assess the *construct validity* of a measure (and is the opposite of *convergent validity*).

Discussion (lab report) For many this is the most exciting element of the research report (no, really!) because it provides, as a starting point, a review of the current literature in the light of the findings of the current study. So this is where you *really* see how your research has added to the whole story in your area of interest! It will start with an overview of your own findings and will then show how these fit in with the research and theory discussed in the literature review. In that way it contextualizes what you have found. Another important element of this section is to review the study and to comment on any strengths or limitations in the design which may lead to ideas and suggestions for future research. So, a helpful hint: if you are trying to decide on a dissertation topic, it is the latter part of the Discussion section in other researchers' work which may give you some great ideas!

Dispersion—see *Measures of dispersion*

Distribution The clue is in the name here! Distribution is about how your data are distributed or spread out. Sometimes your data may be all jumbled up, and other times they may have a distinctive shape (see *normal distribution* or *bell curve*, as well as *leptokurtic distribution, platykurtic distribution*, and *positive and negative skew*). It is important because the type of distribution you have impacts on the kinds of statistical analyses you can use.

Double blind testing This is an experimental procedure in which neither the researchers nor their participants know which condition of the study the participants are taking part in (i.e. either the experimental or the control group). It is used in order to avoid possible bias in the results. For example, some psychologists have been asked to test whether a new brand of cola is as tasty as the leading brand. They employ a research assistant to dispense the products without telling them which is which, so they can't pass on any of their own expectations to the participants, either consciously or otherwise. Additionally, the participants are not told which

D

product they are tasting (though they may have a good idea!)

> Student Says ... Think of a double blind study (where neither the experimenter or the participant know the full nature of the study) as a person with both eyes closed, whereas a single blind study (where the experimenter knows the full nature of the study but the participant doesn't) is a person with one eye shut.

Double Blind

Single Blind

Double hermeneutic This term relates to a two-stage interpretation process used by qualitative researchers. To achieve an understanding of information regarding some aspect of life, the participant will provide an account of their experience—the first stage. The researcher will then try to make sense of what the participant has said—the second stage. So the researcher (interpretation two) is making sense of the participant's own sense-making processes (interpretation one). This indicates the two-way relationship between the researcher and the researched. FYI—hermeneutics is just the branch of knowledge that deals with interpretation.

DV—see *Dependent variable*

Ecological validity This type of validity
refers to how well a study reflects what people
do in real life. So assessing everyday memory in
a laboratory by asking participants to recall previously learnt lists of words may not be as relevant to everyday memory as the more real-life
question as to how people remember where they
parked their car! It also refers to how well the
results obtained from participants in a study can
be assumed to reflect what would be found in
any other group of participants. For example, a
study using 20-year-old university students may
not be 'generalizable' to all 20-year-old people.
This is a form of *external validity*.

Effect size An effect size is a standardized
measure that tells us how big (or how important in practice) the difference is between two
or more groups. So whereas *significance* tells
us whether there is a statistical difference that
we can be confident is not due to chance, effect
size tells us whether we should care about it!
For example, you might read that there is a significant difference in health outcomes between
people in the North and South of England.
However, if the effect size is tiny we would not
need to be concerned about that as it would
suggest that the difference was of very little,
if any, practical relevance. Effect size is good
because, unlike tests of statistical significance,
it is not affected by the size of the sample. The
actual measure used depends on the analysis

being carried out, but measures include *Cohen's
d*, *Eta squared*, and *Pearson's r* (that's right, the
correlation coefficient is also a measure of effect
size!) A historical note: at one point a journal
would have been happy simply to hear about
significance. Not so any more! Most journals
now will be as interested in effect sizes as they
are in significance, so you will need to get to
grips with this. See Table C on page 107 for lots
more lovely information.

Eigenvalue In *factor analysis* eigenvalues are
used to determine how many factors (groups of
items) are needed to interpret the underlying
(latent) variable. It is reported as a number, and
anything less than 1 is not generally considered
to represent a meaningful factor. An example might help here. So, if we are interested
in 'love' as the *latent variable* (overarching
variable), eigenvalues might allow us to see that
the different factors of 'love' could be 'familial
love', 'love of friends', 'sexual love' etc. In this
case, each factor would be made up of number
of items (e.g. familial love = '*I enjoy spending
time with my siblings*', '*my parents mean a lot to
me*', '*spending time with family is important to me*'
etc). An eigenvalue tells us how much of the
variation in the *latent variable* is accounted for
by any particular factor.

Empirical Empirical is a term which sounds
scary but simply means that something (for
example, research, a study or a paper) is based

E

on observation or experience rather than theory. So, for example, an empirical study would be a study that has actually investigated an issue (through the collection and analysis of data) as opposed to simply theorizing about it.

Empirical probability Essentially all this means is the number of times something actually occurred compared to the number of times it could have occurred. An often-cited example: imagine you want to assess the empirical probability of throwing a head when you toss a coin ten times. You toss the coin ten times and you record the fact that six of the throws turned up a head, or you have six 'successful' throws. Empirical probability is therefore 6:10, i.e. a head came up six times out of the ten times that it could have. Probability is recorded between 0 and 1 with 0 being no 'successes' to 1 being 100% 'successful'. In our example, the empirical probability would be .6 or 6/10.

Empiricism This term relates to a research approach that relies on observations and experiments and, as such, forms the basis for the scientific method used in research. It originated from John Locke, a seventeenth-century philosopher, who believed that the only way we gain knowledge is through our senses (rather than through logical argument).

Epistemology This term comes from a branch of philosophy and quite literally means 'the study of knowledge'. It is concerned with what knowledge is, and it refers to how we produce knowledge, what we know, and how we know what we know(!). In qualitative psychology, it relates to a position we take to help create appropriate research questions based on our own understanding of the world, and subsequently to make sense of any data produced (regardless of whether that's in the form of an interview transcript, video etc.). So, for example, some philosophers might argue that knowledge can be found from simple logical thought, whereas others might argue that knowledge must be derived from the testing of specific hypotheses.

Error bars Error bars are used to enhance the understanding of various types of graphical display, including *bar charts, histograms, scatterplots*, and so on. They do this by showing how much uncertainty or *variability* (hence 'error') there might be in a given dataset, given that the measurement for a *sample* would be unlikely to be exactly the same as that of the *population*. The error bars will normally represent either the *standard deviation*, the *standard error*, the *confidence intervals*, or the *range* of values in a dataset. As you might expect, the length of the lines

Figure 12 Error bars

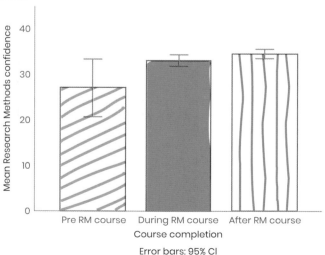

Course completion

Error bars: 95% CI

that extend from the data point will indicate how much uncertainty there is: the longer the line, the greater the uncertainty. An example of error bars in a bar chart can be seen in figure 12 but error bars can be displayed either vertically (as in figure 12) or horizontally, depending on which axis the continuous scale is on, the *x*- or *y-axis*. In figure 12 we can see that there is more variability in 'confidence in research methods' in the 'Pre Research Methods' group (the longer line shows more variability) than in the 'During' or 'Post' Research Methods classes (in which the line is shorter, showing reduced variability).

Error variance We know that *variance* is about how spread out the scores are in a dataset. Error variance is simply the amount of spread in those scores which hasn't been explained by the *independent variables*. An example would be the *within group variance* in an *ANOVA*. You'll sometime see it referred to as random error, random variance, or the residual (the latter because the residual variance is any variance left over that hasn't been explained by the independent variables).

Eta squared $\left(\eta^2\right)$ This is a measure of *effect size* and is reported as a number between 0 and 1 (see Table C, Effect sizes). According to Cohen (1988) .01 is a small effect size, .06 is a medium effect size, and .14 is a large effect size. So if you have an effect size of .03

(a small effect size), it means that only 3% of the variability in the *dependent variable* can be accounted for by differences in the *independent variable*. It works pretty well if you have a fully *between-groups design*, and there are equal numbers in each condition, otherwise, see *partial eta squared*. Just one more thing (if you're still interested), eta squared is similar to the *coefficient of determination* seen in *correlations* and *regression analyses*.

Cohen, J. (1988). *Statistical power analysis for the behavioural sciences.* (2nd ed.) New York: Academic Press.

Ethics Ethics, as defined by the British Psychological Society, are moral principles which guide the way research should be conducted, from the design stage, through completion, and then on to publication of findings (see figure 13, and Table D at the end of the book). These are distinct from laws which provide strict rules and regulations in research, including, for example, the Data Protection Act, the Human Rights Act and so on. Ethical guidelines are designed to help researchers conduct their research in a way that has due regard for the psychological and physical well-being of both human participants and animals.

British Psychological Society (2010). *Code of human research ethics.* BPS publication: Leicester.

Figure 13 Ethics

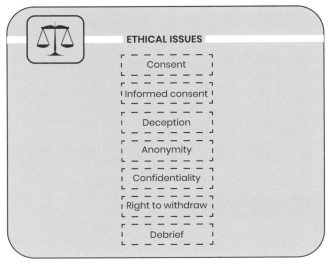

E

Ethnography This is a type of research where the focus is on people and cultures. When conducting ethnographic research, researchers immerse themselves in a particular social setting (e.g. a hospital ward) or within a particular social group (e.g. the Hadza, hunter-gatherers in Tanzania), so that they can observe events and behaviours directly in their natural setting. They would use a scientific, systematic approach to record what they see. The term 'ethnography' is also used to describe the results of ethnographic research.

Expected frequencies An expected frequency is the number of times you would predict that something is likely to happen, based on what we know about the variables under consideration. For example, before throwing a die, you might predict (expect by chance) the frequency of any number turning up to be 1 in 6. In a *Chi-square* test expected frequencies are compared to actual *observed frequencies* to establish whether the data are significant or not. As an example, we could question whether there is an association between type of dog treat (meat or biscuit) and whether or not the dog obeys an instruction (obey or not obey). The expected frequency would be the numbers of dogs expected in each condition assuming that the type of treat offered had no impact on behaviour. Table 5 shows what we might have expected in brackets next to the actual observed frequencies. You could then run a Chi Square test to compare the frequencies to see if there was a significant association between them.

Experimental condition In experimental research the aim is to manipulate one or more variables (the *independent variables* or *factors*) to see whether that manipulation has any effect on the *outcome variable* (the *dependent variable*). Medicinal examples always help here! If a pharmaceuticals company wants to test out its new wonder drug for an exercise-free six pack, they could expose one group, the experimental condition, to the new drug, and another group, the control condition, to a placebo (maybe a sugar pill) instead. Any significant difference in six packs observed could be attributed to the new drug.

Experimental design An experimental design is a research design which involves the manipulation of one or more variables (the *independent variable* or *factors*) to assess the impact of this manipulation on the *outcome variable* (the *dependent variable*). For that reason experimental designs try really hard to control any other factors (*extraneous variables*) which might also impact on the dependent variable because, ultimately, the researcher wants to be able to say whether or not their manipulation caused any change seen in the dependent variable (or, put another way, they want to assert cause and effect).

Experimenter effect The experimenter effect is a type of unwanted influence on the participant within a study which may be created by the researcher. This could include things such as tone of voice or body language, but whatever it is, it confounds the results of the study. For that reason, researchers may consider asking a Research Assistant to conduct the study for them, providing them with the information about how the experiment is to be conducted, but not with the hypothesis behind it (in other words, the research assistant is blind to it).

Experimental group—see *Experimental condition*

Experimental hypothesis When we conduct a study we predict that we will find certain outcomes based on prior research. This prediction is stated formally as the experimental or *working* or *alternate* or alternative(!) *hypothesis*. Occasionally you may see this hypothesis represented by the symbol H_1 which would stand for hypothesis one (you may, of course, have a few). By the same token, the *null hypothesis* would be represented by H_0.

Experimental research A type of research in which we manipulate *variables* in order to determine cause and effect. It is worth noting, here, the distinction between experimental and *correlational research*, the latter here involving no manipulation of variables (and therefore

Table 5 Expected frequencies

	Meat	Biscuit
Obey	60 (41.4)	35 (53.6)
Not obey	25 (43.6)	70 (56.4)

not establishing causality). Compare with *quasi experiment*.

Explained sum of squares The *explained sum of squares* is a measure of how much variation in the *dependent variable* was explained by your model. The larger the explained sum of squares, the better your model fits the data. You might also want to see *residual sum of squares*.

Exploratory factor analysis—see *Factor analysis*

External validity External validity relates to both how well the results of a study can be generalized to naturalistic, everyday settings, and how well they relate to other people, other places, and/or other times. In terms of generalizing to naturalistic, everyday settings, a study on memory with good external validity would be interested in how you remember items to buy in your supermarket shop as opposed to how you remember any old list of words in a lab! In terms of how well it can relate to other people, other places, and/or other times, if we tested a group of undergraduate students on their dietary preferences during their first year of study, could we be sure that the results would reflect the preferences of *all* first year students in that university, or the preferences of those *same* students the following year? If not, we would not have external validity.

Extraneous variable An extraneous variable is any *variable* other than the variables which you are studying which might have an impact on your outcome. They are generally unwanted but are not necessarily a disaster. Why not? Let's take an example. If you want to test the time taken to run 100m before and after a rigorous training regime, baking heat would slow the runners down. But if it is baking hot in both conditions, before and after, the researcher can still see the impact of the intervention, even though the outcome variable has been affected. When it really DOES matter is when you have a special kind of extraneous variable called a *confounding variable*. As the name suggests, this confounds your results!

Student Says . . . I remember what things could be extraneous variables by thinking of the acronym 'ESP'. Experimenter (for things like their gender), Situational (for things like noise and temperature) and Participant (for things like their age or their intelligence)

E

F-ratio You might also see this referred to as the *F*-value. It is the number that represents the share of the *variance* between-group scores *(between-group variance)* in relation to the variance in scores within each group *(within-group variance)* (. . .What on earth?) Put (hopefully!) more simply, if you want to understand differences between two or more groups of data, regardless of whether those data come from a within- or between-groups design, you need to take into account the fact that there will also be individual differences in the scores of the people within any one group (variance within the groups of data). The *F*-ratio divides the between-group variance by the within-group variance. In calculating this ratio, the *degrees of freedom* in the study are also taken into account

in order to determine how significant the results are. The lovely diagram in figure 14 may give you some more help in understanding this.

The *F*-ratio is used when reporting *ANOVA*, as well as when considering *simple regression* and *multiple regression*. As a point of interest (well, we, think so!), it is named after Sir Ronald Fisher, the man who invented ANOVA—hence the use of the letter 'F'.

Face validity This is the most basic form of validity—but a very useful first step! A measure is said to have face validity if, simply by looking at the content (e.g. items in a questionnaire) it appears to make sense. For example, in a happiness questionnaire items such as 'life is good' and 'I laugh a lot' would appear to reflect happiness.

Figure 14 *F*-ratio

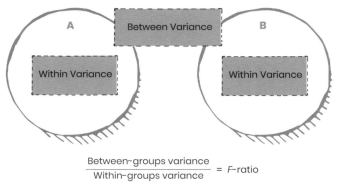

$$\frac{\text{Between-groups variance}}{\text{Within-groups variance}} = F\text{-ratio}$$

> **Student Says . . . There are so many different types of validity but the easiest one to remember is 'Face Validity' if you just think 'On the face of it, this measure looks good.'**

Facilitator A facilitator is used in *focus groups* (or a group of people recruited to discuss a specific issue) in order to 'facilitate' or encourage interaction and discussion between them. They may also be called a *moderator*.

Factor Rather confusingly, there are several different uses of this term (oh good!). In *analysis of variance (ANOVA)* 'factor' is just another name for an *independent variable*, while in *factor analysis*, it is used as a substitute term for a *latent variable*. As if that weren't enough, a factor is also a number by which another number is multiplied (e.g. if birth-rate doubled, it would have increased by a factor of two) and it is also a number that divides precisely into another number (e.g. 2, 3, 4, and 6 are all factors of 12, because the result is a whole number)!

Factor analysis Factor analysis is a statistical procedure which allows us to identify the important underlying dimensions (or *factors*) of more complex phenomena which, in themselves, cannot be directly measured. It does so by looking at the way all of the *observed variables* interact with each other (*observed variables* meaning the variables that you, as a researcher, have measured). As an example, a Travel Agent might use Factor Analysis to understand the factors behind a customer's choice of one of their holidays. These may include 'broad choice of accommodation', 'broad choice of flights', 'affordability', 'ease of booking', etc. (I am told the 'etc.' should definitely include use of WiFi, but I'm not convinced!) Factor Analysis will group items (variables) into factors and will let you see which of the factors are more important than others: for example for the factor 'affordability', items could include 'good choice of cheap hotels' or 'broad range of budget car hire options'. Last thing to know! There are two types of factor analysis—*exploratory factor analysis* (for when you really have no clue how many factors there might be in a set of variables), and

confirmatory factor analysis (for when you *do* have a clue about how many factors there might be in a set of variables, and you simply want to 'confirm' it).

Factor loading *Factor analysis* is a statistical procedure which produces clusters (groups) of items or *observed variables* which are closely related to one another and help us to explain an overarching (*latent*) *variable*. The relationship of each item to the latent variable is expressed by the factor loading (the correlation between the individual item and the factor). Where there is more than one underlying factor, these values can help you to interpret the factors. For example, in a study looking at intelligence, if items relating to problem solving have higher loadings (*correlations*) on factor 1, and items relating to general knowledge have higher loadings (*correlations*) on factor 2, we could interpret factor 1 as representing Fluid Intelligence and factor 2 as representing Crystallized Intelligence.

Factorial design When you want to test the difference between the effects of two or more variables (known as *factors*) and multiple groups (known as *levels*) all at the same time, you are looking at a factorial design, and the statistical technique you would use here is *Analysis of variance (ANOVA)*. Figure 15 shows an example of a factorial design where a researcher wants to know whether a person's role in a company (Factor 1—Job Role; levels—administrator and salesperson) and the type of company they work for (Factor 2—Company type; levels—car dealership and clothes store) might have an effect on their workplace satisfaction (the *dependent variable*). The analysis is based on the mean scores for each group involved, and it is an extension of the *t-test*, which can only manage analysis of two sets of data. You could also look at *one-way ANOVA* for a comparison.

False negative—see *Type II error*

False positive—see *Type I error*

Falsification One of the basic principles of scientific research is that any research *hypothesis* (or question) should be testable and at least be capable of being found to be wrong—the falsification principle. It is based on Karl Popper's premise that you can never be 100% sure about

Figure 15 Factorial design

| Car dealership - Administrator | Car dealership - Salesperson |
| Clothes store - Administrator | Clothes store - Salesperson |

anything (google 'black swans' if you don't believe it!). If not falsified on testing, a scientific statement can then be supported. Scientists would not, therefore, accept questions like 'Is there a god?' as a scientific question as God's existence can't be disproved.

Family-wise error If we perform multiple analyses on the same set of data we increase the risk of finding a significant result (even if one doesn't really exist!—see *Type I error*). To address this problem there are several tests that can be used (see *post hoc tests*). These 'tweak' the significance level behind the scenes, making it a little bit less likely that we will falsely claim that we have found a significant result when we haven't.

Fatigue effect If participants in a study are asked to repeat a task more than once, or to do several similar tasks, they can get used to the content of the task and/or the procedure, and this can influence their performance. For example, people may become slower at

recognizing faces in a facial recognition task as a result of tiredness or boredom, and this is known as a fatigue effect. So, researchers should be aware of this at the design stage and avoid the situation wherever possible, perhaps by allowing sufficient time between testing or using a *between-groups design*.

Field notes In *qualitative* research it is important that the researcher keeps an accurate, descriptive, and detailed account of everything that happened as part of their research, how they felt, and what they thought about it, and perhaps also how they responded to it. For this reason the notes will contain both elements of description as well as reflection. These field notes are then used to provide evidence for the meaning and understanding reached by the researcher of an event, situation, or phenomenon, either in isolation or in addition to, perhaps, *interview* data.

Field study In a field study, people are observed behaving spontaneously in an 'everyday' setting, whether that be in a school playground, an office, a hospital waiting room, etc. but, importantly, the researcher has control over the *independent variable (IV)*. A lovely example of a field study was one conducted by Hofling et al. (1966). Their aim was 'To create a more realistic study of obedience than Milgram's by carrying out field studies on nurses who were unaware that they were involved in an experiment'. So, they conducted their research 'in the field' (in this case on a hospital ward), but they were able to manipulate the information that nurses received to see how that might affect their decision-making processes. If you don't know this research, look it up—it is a highly revealing study!

Hofling, C. K., Brotzman, E., Dalrymple, S., Graves, N. & Bierce, C. (1966). An experimental study of nurse–physician relations. *Journal of Nervous and Mental Disease, 143*, 171–80.

Fisher's exact test Like the *Chi Square* test, this is an *inferential test* that is used when we want to investigate whether there is a statistically significant association between two *categorical variables*. It is used when the *expected frequency* is too small to be used in a Chi Square (and you'll only know that once you have run the Chi Square analysis). BUT, don't let the name fool you, it's no more exact than any other test!

Floor effect This describes what happens when a measure is not sensitive enough to capture a range of scores, and the majority of scores recorded are clustered at the lower end of the scale or are the minimum score. For example, researchers might want to assess the health state of a group of people over a period of time. If the initial assessment found that scores on a 'perceived health questionnaire' were all very low, subsequent tests using that questionnaire would not allow for any further deterioration to be picked up. See how this compares to a '*ceiling effect*'.

Focus group This is an approach used in qualitative research to collect data. It involves a group of deliberately selected people (typically somewhere between 4 to 12, although too many can be hard to manage) taking part in a discussion focused on a specific topic. The discussion is managed by someone called a *moderator* or *facilitator*, who introduces relevant issues and manages the group dynamic. The focus group discussion is recorded (and sometimes videoed) for later analysis.

Frequency Frequency is another name for a tally, or count, when looking at *categorical data*, or the number of times an event occurs. For example, we could take the frequency of females under 25 who play rugby, or we could take the frequency of times that the United Kingdom has won the Eurovision Song Contest (have we ever won the Eurovision Song Contest?)

Frequency distribution This simply means how many times a particular score or variable is represented in a data set. For example, the frequency distribution of the favourite pet of 40 people might be 14 cats, 15 dogs, 8 rabbits, 2 guinea pigs, and 1 marmoset where 14, 15, 8, 2, and 1 are the frequencies.

Friedman's ANOVA This is an *inferential test* that is used when we want to investigate whether there is a statistically significant difference between three or more related groups of people (a *dependent, repeated* or *within-groups design*). Friedman's ANOVA is the *non-parametric* equivalent of the *repeated-measures ANOVA*, and it would be used if we have *ordinal data* or when the data do not meet parametric assumptions. So, for example, Dr Umami might be interested in comparing taste ratings (note that this is ordinal data—'mmm, like this a lot' to 'yuk, this is revolting') across three different types of food (our three conditions): sweet, sour, and savoury.

F

Generalization Generalization is one of the main targets of scientific research and refers to a process by which researchers draw conclusions about their group of interest (the *population*) from the group of people who represent them (their *sample*). In order to be able to say that what is true of a restricted number of people in a research project is also true of all people in that population, researchers have to be very careful about their *sampling* rigour, the *validity* and the *reliability* of their measures and so on. If researchers aren't careful then the conclusions they draw from their sample can only really be conclusions about that sample and can't be generalized to the larger group.

Goodness of fit Goodness of fit tells you how well the actual data collected fit a model or an equation. In other words, how well did the data that were *actually* collected fit the pattern that the model or equation predicted? Chi Square is the most commonly used 'goodness of fit' test, but others include *Kolmogorov Smirnov*, Anderson-Darling, and Shapiro-Wilk.

Greenhouse–Geisser When we conduct a within-groups *ANOVA*, it is important to check that the spread of scores (*variance*) between each pair of conditions is approximately equal (i.e. '*sphericity*'). When this is not the case, a Greenhouse-Geisser correction can be applied to the data to ensure that they are still meaningful. Behind the scenes it does this by 'tweaking' the *degrees of freedom* before calculating the *F-ratio*, in order to provide a more conservative significance value (i.e. a lower alpha level). The important thing to note is that the Greenhouse-Geisser correction deals with this statistical difficulty so that we can be confident that the results are meaningful. Details about this can be found in the paper.

Greenhouse, S. W., & Geisser, S. (1959). On methods in the analysis of profile data. *Psychometrika*, 24, 95–112 but remember, when this was written SPSS did not exist, so calculations were done manually!

Grounded theory Grounded theory uses an *inductive* research methodology which involves the systematic collection and analysis of *qualitative* data from which an explanatory theory is constructed. More generally, you can think of it as any theory which is grounded in (or based on) data. Rather confusingly, perhaps, it is also both the process ('We used grounded theory as the way to reach our conclusions') and the end point ('This grounded theory was achieved through the collaborative input from the members of our team').

Hawthorne effect When participants take part in research they sometimes change their behaviour in a positive way simply because they know they are being studied. This tendency to modify some aspect of behaviour due to an awareness of being observed is known as the Hawthorne effect. It gets its name from a famous set of studies conducted at the Western Electric factory in Hawthorne, Illinois in the late 1920s and early 1930s, where, regardless of changes in working conditions, productivity improved due to the presence of researchers. You may be interested in looking at the *Pygmalion effect*, too.

Helmert contrast This is a type of *contrast analysis* used in the *analysis of variance* which compares the *mean* for each *level* of a *factor* to the mean of all subsequent levels. It is used when the levels are in a meaningful order—e.g. a test of 'easy', 'medium' or 'hard' questions.

Hermeneutics This term relates to the theory of interpretation, and is a methodology used by qualitative researchers to make sense of data gathered from participants. For example, the transcript of an interview will be interpreted by the researcher in order to make sense of the underlying meaning of what has been said, and this may differ according to the personal experiences, beliefs, attitudes, and background of the researchers involved.

Heterogeneity of variance Heterogeneity of variance describes an unequal spread of data

(*variances*) in *samples* that have been drawn from a *population*. In the *scatterplot* in Figure 16 (and you can compare it with the scatterplot for *homogeneity of variance* in Figure 20), the mean number of words recalled is clearly higher using an image-linking technique than a rehearsal technique, but also, and importantly, the distribution of the scores used to create the mean is quite different, with there being much less spread in the rehearsal technique group than in the image-linking technique group—in other words, they have heterogeneity of variance. You can compare this with *homogeneity of variance*, *homoscedasticity*, and *heteroscedasticity*.

Heteroscedasticity It might help to know that this term comes from the Greek *heteros*, which means different or other, and *scedasticity*, which means to scatter. So, it refers to the situation where the pattern in the spread of scores (*variance*) around the *regression line* for the *outcome variable*, is not the same for all values of the *predictor variable*. Heteroscedasticity is a problem in *regression analyses* as the spread of scores needs to be similar or the same for all values of the predictor variable. If you look at the diagram in Figure 17 you can see that the spread of scores around the regression line is greater in the bottom left than the top right. See how this differs from *homoscedasticity*.

Histogram This is a visual way of describing a large amount of *continuous* (*interval* or *ratio*) *data*. Each bar in the chart represents a different point along the scale for any given variable (e.g. age)

Figure 16 Heterogeneity of variance

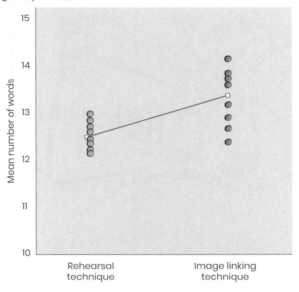

and the height of the bar tells us how often each of those points is represented in our data set (the *frequency distribution*). Because the points are on a continuous scale, all possible points should be represented in the graph, and the bars should touch each other. Where no point is represented in the data, a gap should appear. If you look at the example in the graph in Figure 18, you will see that in a group of 200 students aged 11 to 19, there were no 16-year olds.

Figure 17 Heteroscedasticity

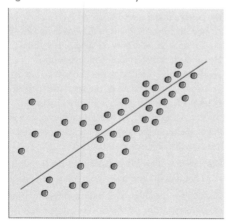

Homogeneity of regression slopes When conducting an *analysis of covariance*, homogeneity of regression slopes is one of the assumptions that needs to be in place. It means that when we interpret the *main effect* for the *between-groups variable*, we need to be sure that there is not a statistical *interaction* between the covariate (CV) and the IV (that would make it really difficult to interpret!). Fortunately, this is easily tested by ensuring that the interaction between the IV and the CV is not significant. However, we do need to know that the *relationship* between each group and the covariate is similar. For example, if we had a positive relationship between Group 1 and the covariate, then we would want a positive relationship between the covariate and all other Groups. To illustrate this, in the following example a researcher is looking at levels of life satisfaction (DV) for different age groups—young, middle-aged, and older age (IV), controlling for income (CV). If we plotted the relationship between the IV and CV for each age group we might see the results shown in Figure 19. We can also test this statistically by looking at the relationship between the covariate and the independent variable (you do not want there to be a significant result!)

Figure 18 Histogram

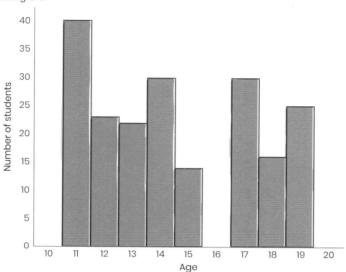

These scatterplots suggest that there is a positive relationship between income and life satisfaction for both the middle-aged and older-age groups, but not for the young age group. Because there is some inconsistency between the different groups, it means that homogeneity of regression slopes has not been achieved.

Homogeneity of variance Homogeneity of variance describes a similar spread of data (*variances*) in *samples* that have been drawn from a *population* and is one of the assumptions of *parametric tests*. Probably easier when you see it in a graph! In the *scatterplot* in Figure 20, although the mean number of words recalled is clearly higher using an image linking technique than a rehearsal technique,

importantly you can see that the distribution of the scores used to create the mean is pretty much the same—in other words, they have homogeneity of variance. You can compare this with *heterogeneity of variance, homoscedasticity,* and *heteroscedasticity*.

Student Says . . . Homogeneity of variance is a really scary term but then I had it broken down for me—'Homo' means 'same' in Greek and 'geneity' comes from 'genus' which means 'group' or 'type'. So homogeneity of variance just means there should be the same kind of variance, or spread of scores, in your groups.

Figure 19 Homogeneity of regression slopes

Figure 20 Homogeneity of variance

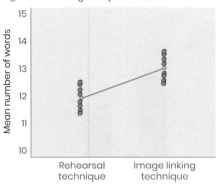

Figure 21 Homoscedasticity

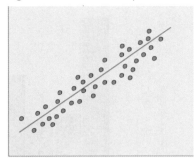

Homoscedasticity It might help to know that this term comes from the Greek *homo*, which means the same, and *scedasticity*, which means to scatter. So it is the assumption that for the *dependent* variable, the pattern in the spread of scores (*variance*) around the *regression line* is similar or the same for all values of the *predictor variable* (see Figure 21). It is one of the requirements for *regression analyses*. See how this differs from *heteroscedasticity*.

Hotelling's T^2 This is one of the *multivariate* test statistics that might be reported when conducting *MANOVA* and it is also called Hotelling-Lawley Trace. It is one of a number of multivariate statistics (see below) and it simply tells us whether the groups in our analysis are significantly different or not (using *eigenvalues* to do so). Hotelling's T^2 is the multivariate equivalent of the *t-test*, so can only be used when the *independent variable* being tested has just two groups (e.g. if you wanted to look at the effect of boys and girls (the independent variable) on two or more variables (your *dependent variables*). The larger the value for Hotelling's T^2, the more likely it is that there is a significant difference between the groups being tested. See also *Pillai Bartlett trace*, *Roy's largest root*, and *Wilks's lambda* for alternative statistics.

Hotelling-Lawley Trace —see *Hotelling's T^2*

Huynh-Feldt correction This is one of the corrections we might consider when assessing the assumption of *sphericity* while conducting a within-groups *ANOVA* where the factor has more than two levels. It is important to check that the spread of scores (*variance*) between each pair of conditions is approximately equal (i.e. '*sphericity*'). When this is not the case, a correction can be applied to the data to ensure that they are still meaningful. Using SPSS, this is done behind the scenes, with the *degrees of freedom* being adjusted before calculating the *F-ratio* in order to ensure a more accurate significance value. The Huynh-Feldt correction is less generous than *Greenhouse-Geisser*, so will provide a more conservative significance value. As a rule, if *Mauchly's test of sphericity* is significant, we would look at the Greenhouse-Geisser correction first, and then consider the Huynh-Feldt correction.

Hypothesis When we conduct a quantitative study we need to make a clear prediction (a hypothesis) about what we expect to find based on what we have learnt from previous research. Specifically, this formal statement of the expected outcome (the hypothesis) should show how two or more *variables* are likely to relate to each other. See also *Experimental hypothesis*, *Null hypothesis*, *One-tailed*, and *Two-tailed hypotheses* for more information.

Hypothetico-deductive method—see *deductive method*

Hypothetico-inductive method—see *inductive method*

Idiographic This term describes a research approach that focuses on the individual rather than a group of people. Within this approach, qualitative methods are used to help us to understand subjective experiences and unique behaviour from a personal perspective. An example of an idiographic approach would be a case study approach. See also *Nomothetic* for an alternative approach.

Independence of data Independence of data is one of the *parametric assumption*s and it is relevant both when you have an *independent groups design* or a *dependent groups design*. In the independent groups design one participant's behaviour or response should not influence the behaviour or response of any other participant. Similarly, in the dependent groups design, although any one participant's responses will be related to each other, the responses between participants should, again, be independent of each other.

Independent ANOVA Also known as a between-groups ANOVA, this term is used to describe the *analysis of variance* used on any design where all of the levels are independent of each other. For example, in a study looking at the effect of IQ (high, average, or low) on problem solving (time taken to complete the Tower of Hanoi task), the data would come from the three different groups of participants.

See *Analysis of variance (ANOVA)* for an explanation of the processes involved.

Independent factorial design Also known as a between-groups factorial design, this term describes an experimental design where there are two or more factors, all of which are independent of each other. For example, in a study looking at the effect of IQ (high or low) and mood (happy or sad) on problem solving (time taken to complete the Tower of Hanoi task), the data would come from different groups of participants—high IQ/happy; high IQ/sad; low IQ/happy; low IQ/sad—making them all independent. See *Analysis of variance (ANOVA)* for an explanation of the processes involved.

Independent groups design—see *between-groups design*

Independent *t*-test This is an *inferential test* which is used when we want to investigate whether there is a statistically significant difference between the means for two groups of data. It is used when different people provide information for each condition and the following are true:

a) the data being used are *interval* or *ratio* (i.e. continuous);

b) the scores we get from participants have a *normal distribution*; and

c) there is *homogeneity of variance*.

The independent *t*-test is a *parametric* test—have a look at the *Mann-Whitney U* test for a non-parametric alternative.

Independent variable (IV) This is a data item which may be manipulated in some way, either by the researcher (e.g. memory technique, the groups being image-linking or rote-learning) or as a naturally occurring 'manipulation' (e.g. parents and children), in order to assess the impact that it has on another variable (called the *dependent variable*). As an example, imagine that a sports psychologist wants to investigate whether a programme for visualization improves performance in the 400m relay. The independent variable is completion (or not) of the programme for visualization. That manipulation is then tested to see whether it has any impact on the outcome (the dependent variable), that being the time taken to complete the race.

> Student Says . . . To remember the Independent Variable or IV, think about how ivy (sounds the same!) can be manipulated around a garden fence, just as you would manipulate an IV in an experiment.

Induction—see *Inductive method*

Inductive method The (hypothetico-) inductive method is a particular approach to the way we conduct research which begins with a researcher gathering data and analysing them before formulating a theory which would best account for the findings. You can think of it as a 'bottom-up' approach as it moves from the specific to a more abstract level, in contrast to the *deductive method* which moves from the abstract to the specific.

Inferential statistics These are the statistics that allow us to draw conclusions about our data, and make inferences about the population of interest from the sample used. By comparison '*descriptive statistics*' are only able to summarize any set of data and do not allow inferences to be drawn from them. So, while we can *describe* our data as having a particular average score, or a particular spread of scores,

the *inferential statistics* allow us to say whether differences or relationships between those data are significant (or not). The results of the tests we use to analyse our data—such as *t-tests, chi-square, correlations, ANOVA*, etc.—all provide us with inferential statistics.

Information sheet So that participants can give *consent* (which may be fully *informed* or otherwise) to take part in a study (an important ethical principle), an information sheet is provided which provides general information that a person might need to know about the nature of the study and their role in it. If full information is offered, the participant can give informed consent; if partial information is given, the participant can give consent on the basis that the missing information would be supplied in the *debrief*.

Informed consent Potential research participants need to be given sufficient information about a research project so that they can decide whether to take part or not. When participants are told precisely what is going to take place in the study they are then able to give fully informed consent. You might be shouting at us now that sometimes it is important to withhold some information so that participants remain naïve to the study and do not alter their behaviour to please (or upset!) the researcher. That's true—if they do choose to take part without full information, they are simply giving their *consent*, and any information that had been withheld would then be provided in the *debrief*. However, please note that this is not the same as *deception*—see entry for more information about that!

Integrity Integrity is an ethical principle which requires that psychologists are honest, fair, and respectful in all areas of their work, whether that be in their research, their teaching, or in their practice. So having integrity means that statements are not made which are misleading or deceptive, and that psychologists practise with a self-awareness that reduces this risk.

Interaction effect This happens when there is a combined effect of two or more *independent variables* on the *dependent variable*. For example, in an experiment where the researcher is looking at differences in the amount of alcohol consumed with regards to student status (student vs. non-student) and personality type (introvert vs. extravert), the interaction effect would reflect the way that student status, *together with* personality type impacts on the amount of alcohol consumed. There are several ways that this might happen. For example, extravert students might drink more than extravert non-students, but there might be no student status difference in alcohol consumption between introvert students and non-students. Have a look at *main effect* for a comparison.

Interaction graph This type of graph allows us to see how two variables are working together. It presents the levels of one factor (IV) on the *x-axis*, and uses the means for each level of the other factor (IV) to create separate lines. The *dependent variable* is represented on the *y-axis*. Although this may sound rather complicated, it is actually a really easy way to interpret the data when an *interaction effect* is found. The graph in Figure 22 shows that extravert students drink more than extravert non-students, but that student status has little impact on alcohol consumption for introverts.

Internal reliability Internal reliability refers to how well and how consistently all of the items in a test (usually in reference to the items in a *questionnaire*) assess the central topic.

Figure 22 Interaction graph

The effect of student status and personality type on alcohol consumption

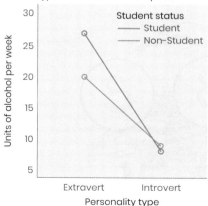

Personality type

For example, if a questionnaire is meant to be measuring self-awareness, and some of the items relate to prospective memory, the scale is unlikely to have much internal reliability. This can be tested using *Cronbach's alpha* or the *split-half* method.

Internal validity This relates to how well the results of a study can be attributed to the effect of the *independent variable* (the variable that is manipulated) on the *dependent variable* (the variable that is measured), so is really considering cause and effect. If we have good internal validity, we can assume that anything other than the independent variable that could have had an impact on the dependent variable (*extraneous/confounding variables*) will have been controlled. For example, in a study looking at the difference in exam scores between first year and final year university students, we would need to take aspects such as IQ and revision time into consideration for the findings to have internal validity. Assessing this type of validity is a way of checking how rigorous the research methods have been!

Interpretative phenomenological analysis (IPA) This is a qualitative approach which aims to explore individual, personal experiences in great detail. When using this approach, the interest is in how people make sense of their own lives, and the processes they might have been through in order to do so. There are two aspects to this approach: the participant's interpretation of their own experience, and the researcher's interpretation of the participant's interpretation! It might help you to understand this if you have a look at the term *double hermeneutic*s.

For more information, see Smith, J. & Osborn, M. (2003). Interpretive phenomenological analysis. In J.A. Smith (Ed.) *Qualitative psychology: A practical guide to research methods* (51–80). London: Sage.

Interpretivism—see *Constructivism*

Interquartile range Used in *descriptive statistics*, the interquartile range is a *measure of dispersion* or spread of scores in a dataset. Specifically, the interquartile range splits ranked data into four equally sized groups (by using three points called *quartiles*) and then takes the middle two groups (or the middle 50%) of the data, with the remaining 50% of the data falling equally above and below this range. It is a useful measure of dispersion as it avoids biases that may come from any unusually large or small scores. Have a look at the *boxplot* (or *box-whisker plot*) in Figure 7 as it shows these quartiles well—the central box is the interquartile range.

Inter-rater reliability This refers to how well two (or more) people rating the same phenomena agree with each other. This is important when scores for behaviours, skills, or performances are being given by attributing numerical values to qualitative evaluations. For example, when Tom Daley dives off the high board, several different judges will allocate a score, and while they might not all be exactly the same, we would hope for a high level of agreement, or high inter-rater reliability, between them (see figure 23). If so, the final mark is reliably indicative of how well he has done.

Interval data Interval data is a *level of measurement* (or a means of measuring data) alongside *nominal* (categorical), ordinal (ordered) and ratio data (data that have been measured on a continuum of equal intervals and have a true zero). It is most like ratio data in that they are also data that have been measured on a continuum of equal intervals—this is why both are sometimes grouped and called *continuous data*. Unlike ratio data, however, interval data have no true zero point and could have a negative value. An example might help! When we report the temperature around the world we might report that it is 0° in Scotland, 10° in the South of England and 20° in the South of France. We know then that it is ten degrees warmer in England than it is in Scotland, and ten degrees warmer in France than it is in England. However saying Scotland is 0° is not saying Scotland has no temperature (it just says you need to get your woollies out!).

> **Student Says . . . Interval level of measurement is a tricky one to remember until you remember that there are 'equal intervals between each value'.**

Interval variable An interval variable uses data that have been measured on a continuum of equal intervals (*interval data*), with no true zero point. Your bank balance would be an interval variable, as a measure of one pound (£1) or one hundred pounds (£100) is on a continuum of equal intervals: if Simon has £300 and Liz has £600, we know that Liz has twice as much money as Simon. Importantly, Harry might have -£150 in his account (i.e. less than zero—unlucky!), which would be five times less than Liz.

Interview In psychology an interview is a focused conversation used to gather data on a particular topic. Have a look at the entries for a *structured interview* and an *unstructured interview* to see the different approaches used.

Figure 23 Inter-rater reliability

Interview schedule When conducting an interview the researcher has a list of questions relating to the topic of interest. They are likely to be *open-ended* to encourage the interviewee to talk in some detail, and this can be further encouraged through pre-considered prompts. This is their interview schedule, and it ensures that all participants are given the opportunity to respond to the same questions during the course of the interview.

Introduction—see *Literature review*

IPA—see *Interpretative phenomenological analysis*

IV—see *Independent variable*

Jefferson transcription This is a very detailed form of *transcription*, often used in *conversation* or *discourse analysis*, where the researcher wants to know not just *what* was said but *how* it was said and sometimes contextual information like scenic background or laughter, too. For this reason the transcription includes all sorts of weird and wonderful signs that, once you understand them, can give you a really good feel for how a conversation, a speech, or the like actually sounded. For example, 'pt' is used for a lip smack, '$' is used for a smile in the voice, (.) is used for a micropause, etc. The system was devised by Gail Jefferson, a co-founder of research using conversation analysis and particularly famous for this transcription system. $—nice one, Gail!

Judgement sampling—see *Purposive sampling*

Kendall's (Tau) correlation Kendall's correlation is an *inferential test* used to assess the *relationship* between two *ordinal* variables (so it's a *bivariate correlation*), and like *Spearman's*, it's a *non-parametric test* (you might compare with *Pearson's correlation*—its parametric equivalent). Which should you use, Spearman's or Kendall's? Well, there's not a huge difference but Kendall's tends to work better with smaller sample sizes, and Spearman's is more sensitive to error, so maybe Kendall's.

Kolmogorov–Smirnov test This sounds as though it should be something to do with vodka tasting—alas it is not. It is a *non-parametric* test that checks to see whether the distribution of scores in a data set is the same, or different, from a *normal distribution* or from another data set. We would be hoping that the distributions are similar, so we do not want this test to be significant.

Kolmogorov–Smirnov Z Once again, there is no vodka involved here (see *Kolmogorov–Smirnov test* if you are already confused!). It is a test that calculates whether two independent groups come from the same population. Like the Kolmogorov–Smirnov test it is a *non-parametric test* and, interestingly, it does pretty much the same as the *Wilcoxon* and *Mann-Whitney U tests*.

Kruskal Wallis test This is an *inferential test* that is used when we want to investigate whether there is a statistically significant difference between more than two unrelated groups of people (an *independent*, or *between-groups design*). The Kruskal-Wallis test is the *non-parametric* equivalent of the *between-groups ANOVA*, and it would be used if we had *ordinal data* or hadn't managed to meet the requirements of a *parametric test*.

Kurtosis The term 'kurtosis' comes from Greek and means 'arched' or 'bulging'. In statistics, the term refers to the shape of the curve seen when a dataset is plotted as a graph. It allows us to know how much of the data clusters around the mid-point of the dataset (i.e. how well the distribution represents a normal curve), or whether there are more bits of data clustered either at the edges of the distribution, or towards the middle of the distribution. The resulting curve can be quite pointy (*leptokurtic*—see Figure 24), meaning that there is not enough variation in the data, or quite flat (*platykurtic*—see Figure 32) meaning that there is too much variation in the data. However, kurtosis is not only represented as a graph, but it can also be understood as a number (oh good!). So, a completely symmetrical, normal distribution would have a value of zero, a positive number means that the curve is too pointy, while a negative number means that the curve is too flat.

Laboratory experiment—see *Experimental design*

Latent variable This is what we call any variable that we assume to exist, but that we cannot measure directly. As psychologists we are interested in all sorts of hidden concepts, such as love, confidence, motivation, sense of belonging, self-belief, intelligence, etc. ('psychological type' variables), but we can't *see* them. So, to measure their existence we need to consider aspects that we *can* see. For example, if we were trying to research 'confidence' we could employ a questionnaire with items such as, '*I feel comfortable meeting new people*' or we could observe participants during a presentation where behaviours (or *manifest variables*) such as speaking clearly and making eye contact with the audience could be considered as indicators of confidence. (Have a look at the entry for *manifest variable* to find out more about this).

Latin square This is a method for allocating participants to different conditions in a within-groups experiment, and the main aim of using this method is to avoid *order effects*. It provides a limited set of different orders that can be used to allocate participants; have a look at Table 6 to see how it works. By the way, it is called a Latin square because the different conditions are represented by Latin letters (rather than Greek ones!).

Table 6 Latin square

	Order of completion		
	1	**2**	**3**
Participant 1	A	B	C
Participant 2	B	C	A
Participant 3	C	A	B

Leptokurtic distribution When the distribution (spread of scores) of our data shows that the majority of scores are clustered in the middle (i.e. around the *mean*), this creates a graph that looks quite 'pointy'. This distribution is known as leptokurtic—from the Greek 'lepto' meaning narrow and kurtosis meaning 'a bulging'. See the entries for *kurtosis* for more information, and for *platykurtic distribution* for a comparison.

> **Student Says . . . If you're trying to remember whether leptokurtic is positive or negative kurtosis, think of leptokurtic as 'leaping up into the air in happiness'! ☺**

Level In *experimental research*, the level of an *independent variable (IV)* refers to the groups

Figure 24 Leptokurtic distribution

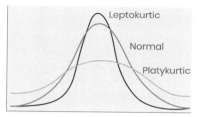

that the IV has been split into (and, in fairness, when there are only two groups we would normally just call them 'groups' or 'conditions'!). Let's take an example. If you wanted to see who can build taller marshmallow towers, engineers or architects, 'occupation' would be the independent variable and there would be two levels, engineers (1) and architects (2). In a *true experiment* the level might be the experimental group (1) and the *control group* (2). Sometimes there might be three or more levels of a variable, in which case we would then call these the levels of a *factor*. An example here might be the factor 'smokers' and the three levels, 'non-smoker' (1), 'smoker' (2) or 'ex-smoker' (3).

Levels of data—see *Levels of measurement*

Levels of measurement The level of measurement of a *variable* (or the characteristic or entity of interest to the researcher) is simply how that variable is measured. There are four possible levels of measurement—*nominal* (or data organized in categories), *ordinal* (or data that have been put into an order), and *interval* or *ratio* (or data that have been measured on a continuum of equal intervals). It is important in statistics as the level of measurement (generally in relation to the *dependent variable*) will tell us what kind of statistical test we can use.

Levene's test When we are looking at differences between groups (in, for example, between-groups *t*-tests or between-groups ANOVA) we need to be sure that the spread of scores (*variance*) in each group is roughly the same, because this allows us to conduct certain statistical analyses. So, Levene's test is a statistical test that checks for this. In other words, it is a test for *homogeneity of variance*—one of our *parametric assumptions*. If we find a significant result for this test it tells us that the variances are significantly different (not what we want), and we would need to consider using a non-parametric inferential test to analyse our data (or, for the between-groups *t*-test, we could refer to the 'equal variances not assumed' line of the SPSS output!). So remember, this is one of the few times when we are hoping to find a non-significant result!

Likert scale The Likert scale (pronounced 'like . . . urt', and named after the man who first developed it, Dr Rensis Likert) is a response format used when conducting *surveys* (or *questionnaires*). It allows participants to indicate their level of agreement with a given statement using an *ordinal* scale. Most often, it is presented as a 5-point scale, which could range from 'Strongly agree' to 'Strongly disagree', but 7- or 9-point scales are also used, and scales can also comprise an even number of points, resulting in a 'forced choice' (ipsative!), where no indecisive option is possible (my colleague in crime, here, loves an ipsative scale! JR). See figure 25 for a 5-point Likert scale.

Figure 25 Likert scale

5-point Likert scale

Strongly disagree	Disagree	Neither agree nor disagree	Agree	Strongly agree
1	2	3	4	5

L

LINEAR MODEL

Linearity Quite simply, a linear *relationship* between two *variables* means that the *data* they provide can be plotted as a straight line. This is important because many of the tests we use can only be used on data that form a linear pattern. So, linearity is one of the assumptions that needs to be in place, and can easily be tested using *scatterplots*.

Linear model This term describes a framework, based on a straight line, which allows us to make assumptions about the *dependent variable* based on known properties of the *independent variable*. It is the most common model used in psychology and it forms the basis of *t-tests, correlations, regression analysis, analysis of variance*, and many other tests.

Linear regression If we want to answer the question 'What is the best predictor of. . .?' then linear regression is the statistical technique to use as this allows us to understand the possible relationship(s) between an *independent variable* or variables (also known as a *predictor variable*) and a *dependent variable* (also known as a *criterion variable*). If, for example, we wanted to consider the best predictor of earning power (that being the criterion variable), we might consider socioeconomic status, IQ, motivation, and adaptability to be prime predictors. These would then be your predictor variables. A *regression* with more than one predictor is called a *multiple regression*. See also *Logistic regression*.

Linear trend A lot of the analyses we conduct in psychology assume that the data will form a straight line when plotted on a graph. This is known as a linear trend. But not all data follow this pattern, so compare this with a *cubic trend*, *quadratic trend*, and *quartic trend*, and see *Trend analysis* for diagram.

Line chart In a line chart, a series of data points are plotted on a graph and a line is then drawn between them to show a trend in the data. For example, an occupational psychologist might be interested in workplace satisfaction, and a starting point could be how salary has differed over the last three decades for men and women. By plotting the average annual salary for each group it would be easy to see any differences that might be present.

Line of best fit The name is a bit of a clue here, as the line of best fit is a straight line drawn on a *scatterplot* that best represents the scores in any data set. It could touch all (very unlikely!) or none (much less unlikely) of the data points, but it tells us something about the strength (how tightly clustered the data points are around the line) and the direction (positive or negative) of the relationship of the data. Have a look at the diagrams in Figure 26.

Literature review (lab report) A component of a lab report/research study, the literature review, in effect, does what it says on the tin! It reviews the literature (both in terms of theory and previous research), in a given area so that having read it, the rationale for the ensuing research is clear. In other words, a good, analytic literature review should be able to show where there is a gap in knowledge, where previous flaws in research may need to be addressed, where authors of previous research have suggested extensions to their work, etc. which will then lead to the rationale and *hypothesis* or hypotheses for the new research. FYI—in a

L

Figure 26 Line of best fit

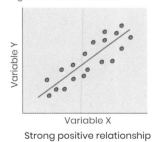

Strong positive relationship

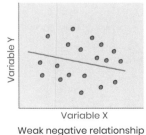

Weak negative relationship

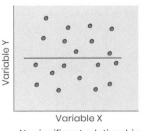

No significant relationship

report this section is sometimes referred to as the *Introduction*.

Logistic(al) regression Logistic regression is a statistical technique that allows us to look at the possible relationship between the *predictor variable(s)* and a *criterion variable*. Importantly, logistic regression is used when the dependent variable is *categorical*. A binary logistic regression would have two categories in their dependent variable (e.g. 'yes' or 'no'). A multinomial logistic regression would have three or more categories (e.g. 'yes', 'no' or 'maybe'). So, if, for example, we wanted to consider the best predictor of likelihood of graduation ('yes' or 'no'—a dichotomous dependent variable), we might consider socioeconomic status, IQ, motivation, and adaptability as good predictor variables. In this case we would be using a binary logistic regression. Logistic regression may also be called Logit regression—the same thing! See also *Linear regression*.

Longitudinal study A longitudinal study is an *observational study* or experiment which takes place over a period of time, rather than on a single occasion. In this sort of study, data are repeatedly collected from the same participants or in relation to the same variable(s). It can extend over several years (e.g. a class of children throughout their primary school years) or even over several decades (e.g. a group of people from childhood into adulthood).

Lower bound estimate This is one of the corrections we might consider when assessing the assumption of *sphericity* while conducting a within-groups *ANOVA*. It is important to check that the spread of scores (*variance*) between each pair of conditions is approximately equal (i.e. '*sphericity*'). When this is not the case, a correction can be applied to the data to ensure that they are still meaningful. Using SPSS, this is done behind the scenes, with the *degrees of freedom* being adjusted before calculating the *F-ratio* in order to ensure a more conservative significance value. The lower bound estimate is extremely conservative and adjusts the *degrees of freedom* for the worst possible case scenario. As such, it is generally considered to be overly harsh and very seldom used. Have a look at *Mauchly's test of sphericity*, *Greenhouse-Geisser correction*, and *Huynh-Feldt correction* for more information about the different corrections that assess sphericity.

Lower quartile Used when describing data, the *quartile*s of a ranked dataset are represented by three cut-points in the data, splitting the dataset neatly into four equally sized groups. The lower quartile (also known as the first quartile) is the lowest 25% of the data, or the data that fall above the bottom edge of a *boxplot* (see Figure 7 which shows these quartiles well).

L

Mahalanobis distances Used in *multivariate analysis*, this is a measure that allows us to determine whether there are any *outliers* in our data which might influence the overall outcome of the study. It is important to check this because a single outlier can have a strong influence on the overall analysis and might affect the *validity* of our findings and our interpretation of the results. So Mahalanobis distances check how far individual scores are away from the average score of the combined predictor variables. The outcome of the analysis is a numerical value. Unfortunately, it isn't possible to provide a single 'cut off' point that tells us when we have an outlier because the outcome is dependent on both the size of the sample and the number of predictors. Fortunately, clever statisticians have created a table of critical values, so all we need to do is look at that to see if the value given for Mahalanobis distance suggests a problem or not!

Main effect A term which is most often associated with *ANOVA*, and is the effect that an *independent variable* has on the *dependent variable*, regardless of the presence of any additional independent variables. So, in an experiment looking at differences in the amount of alcohol consumed within a university setting with regards to status (students vs. lecturers) and personality type (introverts vs. extraverts), there would be a main effect for status—i.e. the difference in alcohol consumption between students and lecturers regardless of their

personality type, and there would be a main effect for personality type—i.e. the difference in alcohol consumption between introverts and extraverts regardless of their status. Have a look at the *interaction effect* for a comparison.

Manifest variable This is the name given to a variable that we can observe, and which helps us to measure a concept that we cannot access directly (i.e. a *latent variable*). Manifest variables could be things like behaviours or physiological responses (e.g. blushing) etc. For example, the *latent variable* of motivation in children could be measured by manifest variables such as their ability to work on a task or complete their homework, or their response to solving a problem . . . or behaviour at failing to do so! All of these manifest variables can be said to indicate the existence of motivation, the underlying (*latent*) variable.

Mann Whitney *U* test This is an *inferential test* which is used when we want to investigate whether there is a statistically significant difference between two unrelated groups of people (an *independent* or *between-groups design*). The Mann-Whitney *U* test is the *non-parametric* equivalent of the *independent t-test*, so is used when (a) is true and either (b) and/or (c) are also true:

a) there is a different set of people in each group (e.g. students and lecturers, or simply a single group of people who have been split into two separate groups)

b) the data being used are *ordinal* (e.g. from a rating scale)

c) the scores we get from participants do not have a *normal distribution* (e.g. in a class test, rather than some people scoring high, some scoring low and most getting somewhere in between, in a test without a normal distribution everyone might get a really high score).

Have a look at *Wilcoxon's Signed rank test* to see more about the test used if the design is repeated.

MANOVA—see *Multivariate analysis of variance*

Marginal frequency distribution Like *marginal means*, marginal frequency distributions (otherwise known, more simply, as 'marginals') are found in the margins of a *contingency table*. They represent the *frequency distributions* of all groups in an *experiment*. Table 7 shows the frequency distributions of teachers and students who have signed up to an on-campus salsa class.

Marginal means Marginal means are found (big surprise here!) in the margins of a table, and they represent the *means* of a group in an *experiment*. Each column and each row will have a marginal mean, which basically means that each *level* of every *factor* will also have a marginal mean. To see this more easily, Table 8 shows the number of sportsmen/women indicating preferences

for team or individual sports. Each factor has a marginal mean for each level, i.e. 'Sportsman', 'Sportswoman', 'Preference for team sports', and 'Preference for individual sports'.

Marginals—see *Marginal frequency distribution*

Matched pairs design A matched pairs design refers to the way an experimenter has allocated their participants to a condition. As an example, 'type of memory technique', as an *independent variable*, might have two levels (or conditions), a 'rehearsal' level and an 'image-linking' level. The researcher has a choice about how they can test this, and one common choice will be to put half of the participants into the 'rehearsal' level and the other half into the 'image-linking' level. This is an *independent design*. However, if the researcher is clever, they may decide that intelligence and age may both influence basic memory, so they wouldn't want, for instance, all older people in one group and all younger people in the other. Instead, they will match the groups so that for every intelligent older person in the 'rehearsal' condition there will be an intelligent older person in the 'image-linking' condition. Likewise, for every 'intellectually-challenged' younger person in the 'rehearsal' condition there will be a similarly 'intellectually-challenged' younger person in the 'image-linking' condition. This

M

Table 7 Marginal frequency distribution

	Signed up	Not signed up	Total
Teachers	45	135	180
Students	64	214	278
Total	109	349	458

Table 8 Marginal means

	Preference for team sports	Preference for individual sports	Marginal mean
Sportsman	32	34	33
Sportswoman	28	12	20
Marginal mean	30	23	

MATERIALS (LAB REPORT)

is a matched pairs design. For other designs, see also *Within-groups design, Related design, Repeated-measures design, Between-groups design, Independent design,* and *Unrelated design.*

Materials (lab report) When you bake a cake you need to know the ingredients and the method used to bake it. Similarly, when you are writing up your research you need to describe your Materials and/or *Apparatus* (your cake-baking 'ingredients'). Your materials will include things like questionnaires, word-lists, pictures of faces and so on. You should provide full information about them, and you should also explain, for example, how you selected the items, and/or reference them appropriately. For example, in terms of describing a questionnaire, you would include the full reference for it alongside, potentially, examples of items within it, information about scoring procedures, reliability, and so on. In terms of how you selected the items you used, if, for example, you wanted to test differences in responses to emotion-laden or neutral words, you would want to report how you chose words of a similar length, number of syllables, and frequency of use. A last comment: just as with Apparatus, don't be tempted to go overboard with photos or images—use them only when they will add to your reader's understanding.

Mauchly's test (of sphericity) This is the test most commonly used to assess the assumption of *sphericity*. We *do not* want this test to be significant, because we do not want the *variance* (spread of scores) between each pair of conditions to be significantly different e.g. if there were three conditions A, B, and C, the difference between A and B should be similar to the difference between B and C, and A and C. If it is found to be significant it means that we can't rely on the *F-ratio* that SPSS (other software is available!) gives us. Fortunately for us, adjustments are made 'behind the scenes' when we run the analysis using SPSS, so if Mauchly's test of sphericity is significant, all we would need to do is report our data from either *Greenhouse-Geisser,* the *Huynh-Feldt correction,* or the *Lower Bound estimate* columns in the SPSS output table! Simple!

McNemar's Chi Square test This is a kind of a *Chi Square* test and you use it when your *variables* are *categorical* (or your data have been organized into groups of some sort). The difference between your usual Chi Square and this one is that whereas in Chi Square your variables are independent (e.g. smoker/non-smoker, driver/non-driver/learner driver), McNemar's is a test for when your variables are related in some way (e.g. before/after studies). So, for example, you could use McNemar's Chi Square if you wanted to see whether there was a difference between the *expected* and *observed frequencies* for a sub-12 second 100 metre sprint (Yes or No) in professional athletes before and after a 'visualization' intervention.

Mean When we talk about the average number of times something happens or the average score in an exam we've just sat, we're actually talking about the mean score. You work it out by simply adding up all of the scores and then dividing that number by the number of scores there are. It is a *measure of central tendency* alongside the *mode* (the most frequently occurring) and the *median* (the middle of a set of scores that have been put in order).

Mean squares (MS) The mean squares is a term for the average *variance* in a set of data. (This is worked out by squaring each score, adding them together, and then dividing by the number of scores—but you knew that!) It is most often seen when you conduct an *analysis of variance,* where it is usually referred to as MS. Interestingly, the *F-ratio* is actually the *between-groups* MS divided by the *within-groups* MS.

Measures of central tendency When we want to describe a set of scores we often want to give an impression of the 'average' or most common scores to give people a 'feel' for the data. We can do this by offering a 'measure of central tendency' which could be either the *mean* (the 'average' score), the *median* (the middle of a set of scores that have been put in order), or the *mode* (the most frequently occurring score).

> **Student Says . . . I could never remember the difference between mode and median until I saw that MOde and 'MOst frequently occurring' share letters in common. MeDian and MiDdle do, too!**

M

52

Measures of dispersion Imagine that you are a teacher and you are reflecting on your pupils' exam scores. To your delight the *mean* score is 80%. What you don't know, however, is whether on average everyone did well, or whether some were excellent and some, well, weren't! To know that you need to have an idea about the spread of scores (as well as the average), otherwise known as the *variability* in scores or their dispersion. Standard measures of dispersion include the *range*, the *interquartile range*, and the *standard deviation*.

Median The median is a kind of average more accurately known as a *measure of central tendency*. If you have a range of scores, to find the median value or score you need to put all of the scores in order and then find the middle score. If there is an even number of scores, the middle two are added together and divided by two. It can be a useful statistic to report when you have extreme scores which are not typical of the other scores.

Memo-writing Memo-writing is sometimes used as another term for *field notes*. It can take on a subtly different meaning in grounded theory, though, as here it is regarded as a step between the field notes and the production of the report. When used in this way as an intermediary stage, the memos are used to reflect on the developing theory as the process of data collection and analysis takes place.

Meta-analysis A meta-analysis is a research method that pulls together the results of a number of studies, all of which have investigated the same issue. It can be really useful when there has been debate over 'what studies say'. For example, there has been much debate over whether or not exposure to violent media predisposes children and adults to more violent behaviour and a meta-analysis can help us to understand the wealth of research in this area. (Guess what—the meta-analysis by Bushman & Huesmann, 2006, found that there *is*, in fact, an overall significant but modest effect for exposure to media violence on varying types of aggression!)

Bushman, B.J. & Huesmann, L.R. (2006). Short-term and long-term effects of violent media on aggression in children and adults. *Archives of Pediatrics & Adolescent Medicine*, *160*(4), 348–52.

Method section (lab report) When you are baking a cake, the ingredients and the recipe are the 'building blocks' needed to bake it successfully (see figure 27). Research methods are the same—they are the specific tools and procedures used in our research to allow us to answer a research question effectively, and the 'recipe' and 'ingredients' should be described in the method section of a report. This would customarily include description of the participants, the materials and apparatus used, the design of the study, and the procedure employed (though a quick flick through any psychology journal will show you that experienced academics may deviate, on occasion, from this norm!).

The detail provided in this section should allow the reader to draw their own conclusions about the reliability and validity of the research, and should also allow others to replicate the study if suitably inspired to do so! Remember that the methods chosen will be influenced by the *methodology*, or the principles that have guided the research.

Methodology The methodology isn't (or shouldn't be!) simply a pretentious way of saying '*method*'. Instead, rather than describing a specific method, methodology is the study of how research is done and how we acquire our knowledge. So, it encompasses a broad range of issues around the generation of knowledge, from the systematic consideration of possible approaches and methods available within a particular discipline, to which specific methods may be best suited to solving a particular problem. For example, a methodological question might be whether to employ a *quantitative* or a *qualitative* approach to the resolution of a research problem. As it is associated with the generation of knowledge we can think of methodology as an *epistemological* issue.

Mixed (between-within) ANOVA A mixed Analysis of Variance is the statistical method used to analyse data that have been collected using a *mixed design* where there is at least one *between-groups* and one *within-groups factor*. You can see the next entry for an example of this type of design. See also *Analysis of variance (ANOVA)* for an explanation of the processes involved.

Mixed design This term describes an experimental design where there are two or more

M

Figure 27 Method section

INGREDIENTS

2 CUPS FLOUR
I CUP GRATED COCONUT
I TSP BAKING POWDER
½ TSP BICARBONATE OF SODA
I PINCH OF SALT
I CUP GRANULATED SUGAR
I CUP BUTTER
I TSP VANILLA POWDER
2 EGGS
½ CUP CHOPPED WALNUTS
½ CUP CHOPPED DARK CHOCOLATE

ROOM TEMPERATURE

BEAT

FLOUR + BICARBONATE + BAKING POWDER + SALT

BUTTER + SUGAR

factors, one of which is between-groups, and one of which is within-groups. For example, a clinical psychologist wants to see how participants' emotional state and type of story affects their recall of emotion-laden vocabulary. They have one group of participants with low anxiety levels and another with high anxiety levels (the between-groups factor). All of the participants (regardless of their anxiety level) read a story about Simon (very happy because everything is going well for him) and another one about Jack (very sad because nothing is going well for him). The 'happy' and 'sad' stories are the within-groups factor. The number of facts recalled from the two stories is the dependent variable. See *Analysis of variance (ANOVA)* for an explanation of the processes involved.

Mixed Methods (Mixed research) Mixed methods research is an approach that combines both *quantitative* and *qualitative* approaches in order to address a research question, and as such it is a type of *multimethod research*. By using these different approaches in either one or a group of studies, it avoids some of the pitfalls of using just the one approach, and therefore gives a more holistic understanding of the topic of interest.

Mode The mode is a kind of average known as a *measure of central tendency* and is simply that score which occurs most often in a dataset.

Model sum of squares—see *Explained sum of squares*

Moderator—see *Facilitator*

Multicollinearity In *multiple regression* analysis, multicollinearity refers to the situation where a high correlation is found between two or more of the *predictor variables*, making it very hard to know which one might be having an effect on the *outcome variable*. Multicollinearity can also be referred to as *collinearity*, and it is one of the issues that needs to be checked when you conduct some of the more complex analyses—e.g. regression. See also *Singularity*.

Multifactorial design A multifactorial design is simply a design where you have 'multiple *factors*', or two or more *variables*. You could have a look at *factorial design* for an example.

Multimethod research A multimethod approach investigates a research question from a number of angles, designing studies which complement each other methodologically and which holistically enable a richer understanding of the research question. For example, a set of studies might employ both within groups and between-groups designs in order to address the pitfalls of both. See also *Mixed-methods* designs.

Multimodal distribution A multimodal distribution refers to a spread of scores which has more than two peaks or modes (a *mode* being the most frequently occurring score in a set of scores). You can compare that with a *bimodal distribution* which would have two peaks. The *bar chart* in figure 28 shows a multimodal distribution as it indicates that the most enjoyed sports are equally football, rugby and fishing.

Multinomial logistic(al) regression—see *Logistic regression*

Multiple Discriminant Analysis—see *Discriminant analysis*

Multiple regression—see *Linear regression*

Multivariate This term simply means that there are many variables involved in the process under investigation. It is most often used to refer to analyses where more than one *dependent variable* or *outcome variable* is being considered, for example, *Multivariate analysis of variance* (*MANOVA*).

Multivariate analysis of variance (**MANOVA**) This is an extension of *ANOVA* (you'll need to read about this first if you're not already clear about the ANOVA element of the MANOVA!), and is a procedure that allows us to consider multiple *dependent variables* at the same time. Using this procedure we can simultaneously look at two or more dependent variables while controlling for the relationship between them.

For example, a researcher might be interested to know whether their super-duper new confidence building intervention improves body esteem (the first dependent variable) as well as mate-seeking behaviour (the second dependent variable) in both men and women. They would therefore be considering the differences in body esteem and mate-seeking behaviour both before and after their intervention (Factor 1: time of testing; levels—pre-test and post-test), and in both men and women (Factor 2: sex; levels— male and female). By the way, you should know that if there is no relationship between the dependent variables, then separate ANOVAs would be more appropriate!

M

Figure 28 Multimodal distribution

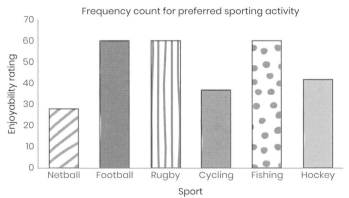

Frequency count for preferred sporting activity

Enjoyability rating (y-axis: 0, 10, 20, 30, 40, 50, 60, 70)

Sport (x-axis: Netball, Football, Rugby, Cycling, Fishing, Hockey)

Narrative analysis This is a *qualitative* research method which has individuals' 'stories' as the key focus. These could be life stories, or they could focus on an event and what that event meant to the individual sharing it, or they could simply talk about everyday experiences. The method for producing the data (whether they are naturally occurring or produced through an interview, written or spoken, and so on) is second, then, to the 'story'.

Natural experiment Things which are of interest to researchers happen every day in the 'real world', whether they be natural, political, economic, or social events. The outcome of these events can be studied, and so form a natural experiment. Importantly, although you cannot manipulate the *independent variable*, you can still look at the effect of a change in the independent variable on the outcome. As an example, a primary school decides to introduce mid-morning snacks as the headteacher believes that this will improve their children's exam performance. A researcher would be able to compare exam results before and after this intervention to see whether this was true. Whilst this type of design has the advantage that people tend not to alter their behaviour as they might in a lab study, it can be difficult to control other factors (*extraneous variables*) which may influence the outcome and therefore any conclusions that are drawn about the study.

Natural study In a natural study people are observed behaving spontaneously in an 'everyday' setting, whether that be in a school playground, an office, a hospital waiting room, etc. but the researcher has no control over the *independent variable (IV)*. Whilst this type of design has the advantage that people tend not to alter their behaviour as they might in a lab study, it can be difficult to control other factors (*extraneous variables*) which may influence the outcome and therefore any conclusions that are drawn about the study.

Negative correlation A *correlation* is a measure of the relationship between two variables. A negative correlation is one where there is an inverse relationship between the variables, or, in other words, as one variable goes up, the other goes down. An example might be, the older a man gets the less hair he will have on his head. See *positive correlation* for the flip side to this coin.

Negative relationship—see *Negative correlation*

Negative skew When the distribution of our data is not symmetrical, and the majority of the scores are clustered to the right of a distribution graph, this is known as a negative skew. Have a look at the entries for *skewness* for more information, and for *positive skew* for a comparison.

Nominal data Nominal data are often called 'categorical data' because they are data that are grouped by category (as opposed to having been organized into ranks or having been measured on any particular scale). The best way to see whether you have nominal data is to ask people which group they belong to. If they can put their hand up to one, and only one, group, and those groups can't be ordered by any sense of size, then you have nominal data. For example, eye colour is nominally scaled because you can't order it and you can't measure it other than simply to count the numbers of people with blue eyes, green eyes, brown eyes, etc. 'Yes' or 'No' as responses would also be classified as nominal data. Be careful, however! If you ask people which group they fall into between: I love research methods/I like research methods/I have no opinion about research methods (there are no other options are there?), this can be put in an order, so although all may have put their hands up to just one group, these are not nominal data! (See *ordinal data* for further enlightenment). Nominal data is a *level of measurement* (or a means of measuring data) alongside ordinal (ordered), and *interval* and *ratio* data (data that have been measured on a continuum of equal intervals).

> **Student Says . . . When you're trying to remember your levels of measurement, it helped me to remember that nominal means 'in name only' so nominal is just about the name of the category (like 'eye colour' or 'favourite food'). Or if that doesn't work, you can just remember the letters in the words are a clue—NAME—NOMINAL**

Nominal variable—see Categorical variable

Nomothetic This term describes a research approach that is concerned with developing general laws or principles that can be applied to everyone. It uses scientific, *quantitative* methods to get objective knowledge which can then be generalized to other people or situations. See also *Idiographic* for an alternative approach.

Non-directional hypothesis—see *Two-tailed hypothesis*

Non-parametric test A non-parametric test is a statistical test that doesn't make any assumptions (e.g. *normal distribution, independence of data, homogeneity of variance*, and that data are at the *interval* or *ratio* level) about characteristics of the *population* from which the data are drawn. Examples of non-parametric tests include *Mann Whitney U test, Wilcoxon's Signed Rank test, Chi Square*, and *Spearman's Rho correlation.*

Non-participant observation This sort of observational research is sometimes known as 'fly on the wall' research as the researcher does not have any direct contact with the group being studied, but simply observes and records 'from a distance'. See *Observational study.*

Non-probability sampling Non-probability sampling does not require that each *participant* (or case) from a *population* has a known probability of being included in the sample (or that we can be sure that they *could* be included within it). Examples of non-probability sampling include *opportunity sampling* and *snowball sampling.*

Normal distribution Normal distribution shows a set of scores that is spread (or distributed) with most of the individual scores centred around the 'average' of all of the scores. There will be fewer and fewer individual scores as you move away from the middle score. For this reason, the spread of scores has a characteristic bell-like shape which gives it its other name, 'the *bell curve*'. It is important as it allows us to understand important properties about the data we have collected. Figure 29 shows a 'normal distribution' of scores in an exam with most people scoring around 80% and fewer and

Figure 29 Normal distribution

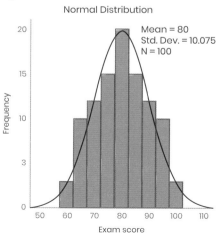

Normal Distribution

Mean = 80
Std. Dev. = 10.075
N = 100

fewer people scoring towards the very high or very low marks.

> **Student Says . . . To remember what a normal distribution looks like I think of a 'paranormal' distribution!**

Null hypothesis When we conduct a study we predict that we will find certain outcomes based on prior research. This prediction is stated formally as the *experimental*, *working*, or *alternate* or alternative(!) *hypothesis*. However, when we conduct an analysis, what we actually test is the likelihood that our variables do *not* relate to each other, and the statement of that expectation is called the 'null hypothesis'. (Note to self! The null hypothesis *is not* the opposite of the experimental hypothesis, it will simply state that there will not be an effect). Occasionally you may see the null hypothesis represented by the symbol H_0 whereas the experimental hypothesis would be represented by H_1 (or H_2 if it is the second experimental hypothesis, etc.)

N

Oblique rotation In *factor analysis* an oblique rotation is a method used to identify underlying *factors*. It assumes that there is a correlation between the factors, and allows for those correlations to be recognized. Have a look at the entry for *orthogonal rotation* for an alternative approach to extracting factors.

Observational study Sometimes a researcher is interested in simply observing behaviour or events and recording what happens in contrast to manipulating variables to see the impact of that manipulation on another variable (i.e. in an *experiment*). There are different types of observational studies—*natural* or *controlled*, *participant* or *non-participant*, and *overt* or *covert*—and any combination of these!

Observed frequencies An observed frequency is the actual number of times an event happens in a study. Generally associated with the *Chi Square* test, observed frequencies are compared to *expected frequencies* to establish whether our data are significant or not. For example, if we were looking at an association between type of dog treat (meat or biscuit) and whether or not the dog obeys an instruction (obey or not obey), the observed frequency could be the actual numbers of dogs seen in each condition as shown in Table 9.

Observed value The observed value is the value you have calculated when you conduct a statistical test, so you could have an observed

Table 9 Observed frequencies

	Meat	Biscuit
Obey	60	35
Not obey	25	70

value of *t* in a *t* test or an observed value of χ^2 in a Chi Square test. You then compare this to the *critical value* for determining whether or not you reject your *null hypothesis*, or, more simply, to see whether you have a *significant* result. Also known as the *test statistic*.

One-sample Chi Square Like all *Chi Squares*, the one sample Chi Square is an *inferential* statistical test used to find out whether there is an association between *categorical variables*, and is tested by assessing the difference between the observed frequencies in our data with the expected frequencies (see *Chi Square* for a bit more!). With a one-sample Chi Square, however, there is only one categorical variable which is checked to see whether it follows a hypothesized distribution. For example, a researcher could ask whether the number of smokers in a group of UK student nurses is equivalent to, or different from, the general UK population. If one in five of the UK population smokes, does one in five student nurses also smoke? The bigger the difference between the one in five (the expected frequency) and the actual data (the observed frequency) in student nurses, the more likely it is that the difference between the two did not occur by chance.

One-tailed hypothesis Sometimes when we conduct a study the literature gives us a clear indication about the way our variables are likely to relate to each other. For example, if we are looking at the relationship between exam success and revision, and the literature shows that the more revision we do, the better our exam results will be (yes, really!), it would make sense to predict that our results would also go in this direction. This would be more informative than just stating that you expect to find that they are related to each other. So this means we make a formal statement, or one-tailed hypothesis, which shows the expected direction of the relationship between our variables. Our one-tailed hypothesis might therefore state, 'There will be a significant relationship between exam success and revision, such that the more we revise the more successful we will be in our exams'. See also *Two-tailed hypothesis*.

> Student Says . . . One and two-tailed hypotheses are easy to remember if you think of a cat sitting on a fence. If the cat's tail is pointing in one direction, then you have a one-tailed hypothesis, you know which direction your hypothesis is going in. If the cat's tail is thrashing backwards and forwards so you're starting to wonder if it has more than one tail, then you have a two-tailed hypothesis and you don't know which direction your hypothesis is going.

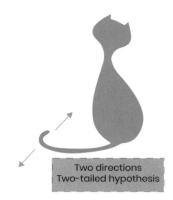

Two directions
Two-tailed hypothesis

One-tailed significance level When we want to know how significant the data from our study are, we are either testing a *one-tailed hypothesis* or a *two-tailed hypothesis* (you might want to read up on this first). A one-tailed significance level tests the statistical significance in the one direction of interest (e.g. the shaded areas of b) and c) in Figure 30). This means that you are testing for the possibility of a relationship or difference in only ONE direction at the .05 alpha level. In this case you're not interested in the relationship or difference in the other direction. Alternatively, if you've conducted a two-tailed test, but want to report the outcome of a one-tailed hypothesis, you would need to divide the *p*-value by two, so you have a significant outcome if your reported *p*-value is less than .025.

One-way ANOVA This is a statistical technique that allows us to test the significance of the difference between three or more groups (known as *levels*) when considering one *factor*. This could be a within- or between-groups design. As an example of the latter, after a particularly over-indulgent holiday, Professor Pike was interested in comparing the effectiveness of three diets—the Atkins diet, the 5-2 diet, and the Cambridge diet. In this case the factor is the diet and the levels were the different approaches that participants were asked to follow. The *dependent variable* here would be weight loss. If Professor Pike had wanted to be really clever she might have controlled for initial weight—see *ANCOVA* for more information!

Ontology Like '*epistemology*', this term comes from the philosophy of knowledge,

One direction
One-tailed hypothesis

Figure 30 One-and two-tailed significance level

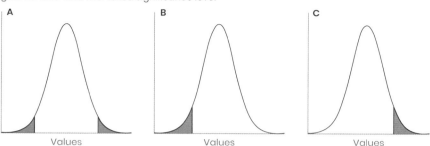

Two-tailed significance can be seen in (A) and one-tailed significance in (B) and (C).

and it literally means 'the study of being'. It is connected to the way individuals see reality, and this may differ from person to person, meaning one person's reality (or knowledge) may not be the same as another person's reality. As researchers we all have our own view of the world and what reality is, and this will affect the way we conduct our research and interpret our data. For that reason it's important that we are clear how we see things, and recognize that others may see them differently. Are you feeling confused? Consider Figure 31. For me, my interpretation of this image is of an old crone.

Figure 31 Ontology

Source: Science History Images/Alamy Stock Photo

For you, you may see a beautiful girl. We *see* the same thing but our reality, our understanding of it, is different. When Hamlet said, 'To be, or not to be' he was having an ontological moment!

Open coding In *qualitative research*, and particularly in *grounded theory*, data are first organized into categories before being organized into a theory or model. It is this first stage of organization that is called open coding.

Open-ended questions When we conduct an *interview* or a *survey*, open-ended questions are those that give the person answering a free choice about what to say. This type of question is used to get people to respond in some depth to the questions about the topic you are interested in, and gives them the freedom to explore areas that the researcher may not have considered. For example: 'What can you tell me about your trip?' would give us a longer answer than 'Did you enjoy your trip?' as the latter is a *closed question* to which the answer could simply be 'yes' or 'no'.

Operationalization This relates to the process of defining the variables used in a study so that they can be clearly measured. By carefully defining both the *independent variable* and the *dependent variable* it means that other researchers can replicate a study accurately. For example, if a researcher was trying to see whether vitamins helped with work, it would be helpful to know what is meant by vitamins—vitamin C, vitamin D etc.—and what is meant by work in this instance (school grades, concentration levels, days off through illness, etc.)

Opportunity sampling (convenience sampling) An opportunity sample is a way of selecting our participants from the group of people we are interested in (i.e. the *population*). Opportunity sampling simply selects those people who are available and willing to take part. It is the least rigorous way of recruiting participants (but is most often the recruitment method used). As lecturers, we are constantly told by students that they used a random sample—they almost certainly didn't! Do have a look at *random sampling* to see what this really means!

Order effects This is a potential problem in a *within-groups design*, where participants take part in more than one task or condition. In this sort of study, the order in which tasks are presented to participants can influence the outcome. For example, if everyone in a study did task A first followed by task B, then it would be hard to know if they are better at the second task because they've got used to doing it (*practice effect*) or worse at the second task because they've got bored or tired (*fatigue effect*)! Have a look at *counterbalancing* for a solution to this problem.

Ordinal data Ordinal data is a *level of measurement* (or a means of measuring data) alongside *nominal (categorical)*, *interval*, and *ratio* data (data that have been measured on a continuum of equal intervals). As the name suggests, ordinal level data means that the data have been put in an order (otherwise known as ranking). For example, we could line everyone up in a classroom by height. Let's say we have 30 people. Each one is given a number from 1 to 30 (shortest to tallest). As the data are arranged in order by height we have more than just nominal (categorical) data, but note we don't know their *actual* height (so we don't have *continuous* data that can be measured on a continuum of equal intervals).

> **Student Says . . .** Ordinal level of measurement is an easy one to remember if you remember that the letters in the words sort of lead you to what it is—ORDINAL means 'in ORDER'

Ordinal variable An ordinal variable is one that is measured using data that can be ranked, or put in order. Educational level could be an ordinal variable as the achievements can be ordered, e.g. GCSE's, 'A' levels, university degree classifications. Other examples are the position of your favourite football team in the league—top, middle, bottom etc., or income levels—low, medium, and high.

Orthogonal rotation In *factor analysis* an orthogonal rotation is a method used to identify underlying *factors* which are not related to each other (uncorrelated). Have a look at the entry for *oblique rotation* for a different approach to extracting factors.

Orthographic transcription Perhaps best explained by defining the words first! So, orthography is the art of writing words using the correct letters according to normal practice. Rather similarly, transcription means the representation of a language in written form and is usually talked about in research terms when we want to transcribe, or write down, the content of an interview. So orthographic transcription uses the spelling system familiar to the researcher to record the content of an interview or focus group. An example could be: < Let's talk about you >. Notice each element uses pointed brackets and has gaps between the words. See also *Phonemic transcription* for contrast.

Outcome variable—see *Criterion variable*

Outlier Also known as an *anomaly*, an outlier is an individual piece of data that represents an extreme score for a particular data set, which can be above or below the expected range. Have a look at the *boxplot* in Figure 7 to see what this might look like.

Overt observation In a study using overt observation, those who are being observed are made aware of the fact by the researcher. This can sometimes influence the type of behaviours displayed, but generally this is a temporary effect and people 'revert to type' before long!

p value—see *Significance level*

Paired Samples *t*-test This is an *inferential test* which is used when we want to investigate whether there is a statistically significant difference between the means for two groups of data. It is used when the same people provide information for each condition and the following are true:

a) the data being used are *interval* or *ratio* (i.e. continuous)

b) the scores we get from participants have a *normal distribution.*

The paired samples *t*-test, sometimes called the *dependent t-test*, is a *parametric* test—have a look at the *Wilcoxon's signed rank* test for a non-parametric alternative.

Pairwise comparisons This term quite simply refers to methods used to assess whether two groups of scores (pairs of *means*) are significantly different from each other. Pairwise comparisons are the basis of *post hoc tests,* where every pair of groups in your study is considered (think 'lots of *t-tests*'!). But remember, when you do multiple tests on the same data you have a problem with increased risk of *Type I error* or *familywise error* so some clever tests such as *Bonferroni's correction* are used to deal with this. However, the bottom line is, pairwise comparisons compare pairs of means.

Paradigm A paradigm is a term used to describe a discipline's way of thinking or 'worldview' at a particular time. It includes issues relating to the theories considered, to how research in the area is carried out, to what constitutes 'valid' research (or not), and so on. Within clinical psychology, for example, we have seen (or are seeing) a paradigm shift from mental health being regarded as separate from physical health, with different training programmes for the two approaches and more resources and treatment options offered for physical health issues, towards, now, a recognition of the need for a more integrated patient-centred approach.

Parameter The parameter is a numerical value that tells us something about our *population* of interest. It could be the *mean* value or the *median* value, the *standard deviation* or the *range*, or it could be a percentage value. It can be compared to the *statistic* that refers to the same numerical value but coming this time from the *sample* of that population (or the particular group drawn from the entire group that you want to consider). As an example, we might be interested in finding the mean age of all undergraduate students studying Research Methods in the United Kingdom. The parameter of this population is the mean age of all undergraduate students studying Research Methods in the United Kingdom. The statistic is the mean age of the 50 undergraduate students studying Research Methods in the United Kingdom that you checked.

> **Student Says . . . To remember that 'parameters' are connected to 'populations' and 'statistics' to 'samples', note that 'parameters' and 'populations' start with 'p' and 'statistics' to 'samples' start with 's'.**

Parametric assumptions For data to be treated as 'parametric' (or characteristic of a *population*) there are certain things which must be true about them, and these are called 'assumptions'. If these assumptions are not met, then we'd have to be a bit careful with regards to any conclusions we draw from our analyses, because we're drawing conclusions based on faulty information, (but there are other analyses that we can use in this situation—see *non-parametric tests*). So what are these assumptions? Well, different tests require different assumptions to be true, but a number of basic assumptions are common to all. Have a look at *normal distribution* of data, *homogeneity of variance*, *interval* or *ratio* level of data, and *independence of data* for more information.

Parametric test A parametric test is a statistical test used when certain 'assumptions' about the characteristics of a *population* have been met. These assumptions may include *normal distribution, independence of data, homogeneity of variance*, and that data are at the *interval* or *ratio* level, and may vary according to the analysis used. Examples of parametric tests include the *t tests, ANOVA*, and *Pearson's correlation*. See also *Non-parametric tests*.

Partial correlation If we are interested in the relationship between two variables, we conduct a *correlation*. But sometimes we also want to take account of other variables that might influence the outcome variable. When we statistically control for (or 'partial out') the effect of one or more other variables the analysis becomes a partial correlation. For example, a health psychologist might want to investigate

the relationship between level of boredom and the number of sweets people eat, but they would also need to take into account additional factors such as current hunger levels and level of self-control. These would be the two variables that would be controlled for as both of these could influence the main relationship of interest.

Partial eta squared (η_p^2) This is a measure of *effect size* most often reported when conducting *ANOVA* (see Table C, Effect sizes). Like *eta squared*, it can be measured between 0 and 1, with .01 being a small effect size, .06 being a medium effect size, and .14 being a large effect size (Cohen 1988). The difference between partial eta squared and eta squared is that whilst eta squared explains the proportion of the *total* variance in the dependent variable that can be accounted for by any one variable (having included the other variables in the computation), partial eta squared only reports the variance in the dependent variable that can be accounted for by a *particular* variable (having excluded the other variables from the analysis). So an advantage that partial eta squared has over eta squared is that you can add more variables to a model without decreasing the proportion of the variance explained by the particular variable you were looking at. Because the proportion of variance explained by a single variable using partial eta squared won't change however many variables are added, it also makes it possible to compare the effect of that variable in different studies. We would also use partial eta squared, in preference to *eta squared*, if the analysis is based on a *within-groups* or *mixed design*, or if group sizes are unequal.

Cohen, J. (1988). *Statistical power analysis for the behavioural sciences.* (2nd ed.) New York: Academic Press.

Partial replication Like a *replication*, a partial replication repeats prior research with the aim of finding out whether the same results will be obtained, using the same techniques, in another *population* or in a different setting. However, in a partial replication, elements of the original study may be changed (e.g. using a *within-* rather than *between-groups* design), perhaps because of theoretical or methodological advances.

Participant observation In a participant observation the researcher becomes part of the group they are studying, or has direct contact with them. Their involvement may be known to the group (*overt observation*) or the group may be unaware that a person in their group is studying them (*covert observation*—which comes with some ethical concerns!)

Participants (lab report) The participants section of a research report describes those who took part in the study. The participants section should report *sampling* methods, i.e. how the participants were recruited (the individuals recruited being known as the sample). You can see the many different types of sampling methods possible in Table E at the back of the book. It should also report any inclusion or exclusion criteria if necessary, and all important demographic characteristics. For example, it would almost inevitably include information about the age and gender of the participants, but it might also include ethnicity or racial group, socioeconomic status, level of education, sexual orientation, and so on. It is up to the researcher to consider which topic-specific characteristics are important to specify. This sub-section is particularly relevant when you are deciding how generalizable the research is. For example, you may notice that many studies describe participants from their university. How generalizable do you think this research is to the wider population? 'Participants', by the way, may be compared with the older term, 'Subjects', which is no longer used as it suggested that individuals do not 'participate in' but are 'subjected to' the research—an important ethical difference!

Participants Participants are essentially the people who take part in our research, and may be compared with the older term, 'Subjects', which is no longer used as it suggested that individuals do not 'participate in' but are 'subjected to' the research—an important ethical difference!

Pattern matrix In factor analysis, the pattern matrix is a rectangular display table which shows the *regression coefficient* for *variables* (think 'items') on every *factor* in the data. This coefficient indicates the strength of the *relationship* between the factor and the items (and it controls for the effect of the other factors on that item). The pattern matrix can be compared to the *structure matrix* which displays the *correlation coefficients* for every *variable* on every *factor* in the data.

Pearson's Chi Square test—see *Chi Square*

Pearson's correlation The full title of this test is Pearson's product-moment correlation, but we usually use the abbreviation! It is an *inferential test* used to assess the relationship between two variables (so a *bivariate correlation*) that have both provided *continuous data* which are normally distributed. So it's a *parametric test* which you might contrast with *Spearman's correlation*—its *non-parametric* equivalent.

Pearson's correlation coefficient This is also known as Pearson's product-moment correlation coefficient (rather a mouthful) or, more succinctly, Pearson's r. It is the number we end up with when we conduct a Pearson's correlation that tells us about the strength and direction of the relationship between the two variables being analysed. The number is a value between -1 and $+1$, where a negative number tells us that as scores on one of our variables change, scores on the other variable change in the opposite direction (a *negative correlation*), while a positive number tells us that as scores on one of our variables change, scores on the other variable also change in the same direction (a *positive correlation*). Have a look at the entry for the *correlation coefficient* for a full description. When we report this coefficient in our results section we use the symbol r.

Percentile In a dataset, the percentile indicates the percentage of data that will fall below a specific point in that dataset. For example, if your newborn baby falls on the 80th percentile for weight, 80% of babies will be lighter than your baby (and 20% will be heavier). Put another way, if your baby is the 2nd heaviest in a group of ten babies, he will be on the 80th percentile for weight.

P

Phenomenology This is a *qualitative research* approach the central aim of which is to understand how people experience and perceive some phenomenon or situation and how they interpret them. The researcher attempts to describe the 'lived experience' of a phenomenon as described by the participant as objectively as possible, using *bracketing* to help achieve this. See also *Interpretative phenomenological analysis*.

Phi This is a measure of *effect size* (see Table C, Effect sizes). Specifically it is a test of the strength of the association between two categorical variables, used when conducting a *Chi Square*. Importantly, it is used when both variables have just two categories (i.e. a 2 × 2 design). You may want to look at Chi Square for more information about the background to this. See also *Cramer's V*.

Phonetic transcription Phonetic transcription is a transcription system (any system which represents a language in written form) which allows you to understand how speech is actually delivered, e.g. pauses, stresses, crossovers in conversation, etc. This type of transcription would be used when a researcher wants to understand more than the actual words but the possible meanings behind how they are delivered. It uses the International Phonetic Alphabet in addition to specific markers which indicate, for example, pause length, inflections at the end of words, etc. See also *Orthographic transcription* for a rather easier transcription system!

Pillai Bartlett trace This is also known as Pillai's trace and is one of the *multivariate* test statistics that might be reported when conducting *MANOVA*. It is one of a number of multivariate statistics (see list at end of entry) and it simply tells us whether the groups in our analysis are significantly different or not (using *eigenvalues* to do so). FYI: it is pretty robust, so it is the best statistic to choose if there are problems with things like unequal groups. The larger the value for Pillai's trace, the more likely it is that there is a significant difference between the groups being tested. See also *Hotelling's T²*, *Roy's*

largest root, and *Wilks's lambda* for alternative statistics.

Pilot study A pilot study is a small scale study carried out prior to a main study in order to ensure that everything works as the researcher thinks it will. It allows different aspects of the study to be tested, for example the design, materials, timings, etc. so that any necessary adjustments can be made before launching into a full scale study with a greater number of participants.

Placebo effect In psychology this term refers to the situation where participants alter their behaviour because they believe they have received some sort of treatment when in fact they have not. It originates from the field of medicine, where some participants in a randomized controlled trial might be given a sugar pill (the placebo) instead of actual medicine, in order to compare the effects of those taking the placebo (should be no effect) with those taking the medicine (probably should be an effect!). Researchers have found that, counter to expectations, placebos can create beneficial effects, which must be due to patients' beliefs, not an actual effect of the medicine (which they're not taking!).

Planned comparisons—see *a priori comparisons*

Platykurtic distribution When the distribution (spread of scores) of our data shows that all the scores are spread out fairly evenly (i.e. not distributed 'normally' around the *mean*, which

Figure 32 Platykurtic distribution

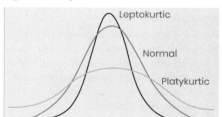

would be a beautiful bell-shaped curve), this creates a graph that looks quite 'flat' (see figure 32). This distribution is known as platykurtic—from the Greek 'platus' meaning flat and kurtosis meaning 'a bulging'. It might help to think of this as a 'plateau' or a 'platypus', both of which have a similar shape! Have a look at the entries for *kurtosis* for more information, and for *leptokurtic distribution* for a comparison.

> **Barbara and Julia say . . .** We like to think of a platykurtic distribution (which is represented by a negative number in the output) as either a platypus (!) or a plateau (?)—we're not going to tell you who prefers which idea! (JR)

Point biserial correlation A point biserial correlation measures the relationship between two *variables* when one has *continuous* data (*interval* or *ratio*) and the other has naturally occurring *binary* data (e.g. dead or alive, student or lecturer, passed or failed). A researcher might, for example, use point biserial correlation to look at the relationship between student and lecturer status, (binary) and earning power (continuous). Incidentally, the correlation coefficient for a point biserial correlation is r_{pb}. See also *Biserial correlation*.

Polynomial contrast This is a type of *contrast analysis* which looks at the *means* for each *level* of a *factor* to establish whether the pattern in the data is *linear*, *quadratic*, *cubic*, etc. It is used when the levels are arranged in a meaningful order (e.g. low, medium, high) and when we want to know the 'shape' of the relationship between them. It can be useful in helping us to decide the best analysis to use to assess *significance* in our *data*, as many of the tests we use are based on a linear pattern.

Population The population is the total group of people we are interested in when we are conducting a research study. So, we might

P

be interested in researching the experience of being taught research methods in all first year Psychology undergraduate students in the UK. In that case the population is 'all first year Psychology undergraduate students in the UK' and our participants will be a *sample* or representative group of them. Note to self—the population does not necessarily mean 'everybody on earth'!

Positive correlation A *correlation* is a measure of the relationship between two variables. A positive correlation is one where as one variable goes up, so, too, does the other. An unfortunate example might be, the older a person gets, the more hair they grow in unwanted places (and why does that happen?)!

Positive relationship—see *Positive correlation*

Positive skew When the distribution of our data is not symmetrical, and the majority of the scores are clustered to the left, this is known as a positive skew. Have a look at the entries for *skewness* for more information, and for *negative skew* for a comparison.

Positivism Positivism is an *epistemological* position, which sounds scary but it just means a particular philosophical approach to the production of knowledge. What approach is it, then? Well, the production of knowledge for positivists is through the collection of observable data and the interpretation of them through strict rules requiring *reliability* and *validity* and allowing *generalizability*. Importantly, too, positivism assumes a *realist* ontology, or put more simply, it relies on the premise that there is a 'real world' out there which exists whether we are consciously aware of it or not! An example? A positivist might argue that 'Criminal behaviour' is a reality that may be researched and understood based upon specific, clearly defined criteria. See also *Relativism* for a different viewpoint.

Post hoc tests The term 'post hoc' literally means 'after this', so *post hoc tests* are those that are conducted after the main analysis. These are not tests that the researcher would have planned before they collected any data, but are used to explore any significant findings further. They do this by comparing the mean scores for each possible pair of groups in the experiment, and because the data are tested on multiple occasions, the significance level for each test tends to be much more rigorous than normal (i.e. behind the scenes the data are considered against a lower alpha level—see *family wise error*). The term 'post hoc test' is a generic label for several different analyses (e.g. Tukey's HSD test, Bonferroni's contrasts, Gabriel's pairwise test etc.), each of which is used under different conditions, but they all follow the same procedure. You may want to compare post hoc tests with a priori tests.

Power (of a test) Power is the probability of avoiding a *Type II error*, i.e. it is the ability of the study to detect a significant finding if one actually exists. Size of *sample* and *alpha level* will both affect power. Note to self—this is not to be confused with mathematical 'power' which is the number of a times a numeral is multiplied by itself (e.g. 8^2 is 8×8, or 4^3 is $4 \times 4 \times 4$).

Practice effects If participants are asked to repeat a task more than once, or to do several similar tasks, they can get used to the content of the task and/or the procedure, and this can influence their performance—for good or bad! So researchers should be aware of this at the design stage and avoid the situation wherever possible, perhaps by allowing sufficient time between testing in order for participants to forget what they have learnt or, if possible, by using a *between-groups design*.

Predictive validity This type of validity refers to how well a particular test or measurement can predict subsequent performance or behaviour. For example, the 11-plus is a test that has been designed to identify students who should do well in a Grammar School. If it has good predictive validity, those students identified should do well when they go to the Grammar School. If they don't, this may be because the test wasn't entirely up to the task. Another example you may be familiar with is the way careers departments use different tests to indicate what sort of job you would be best suited to in the future. It is a type of *criterion validity*.

Predictor variable This term relates to a variable that is similar to the *independent variable* (but it is not exactly the same thing because you don't necessarily manipulate it), and it is most often used in non-experimental or correlational studies. It is a variable that is used to predict the result on an *outcome variable*. For example, a lecturer might use a student's mark on one piece of work (a known value—the predictor variable) to predict the mark on a future piece of work (an unknown value—the outcome variable). Predictor variables are used in *regression analyses*.

Primary source When we gather data for a psychological study we usually want to do so using questionnaires, experiments, observations, etc. This means that the information comes directly from our participants to us, so 'straight from the horse's mouth'! (See Figure 33).

By doing this it means that it might be more valid and trustworthy than if we collected it from a third party. For example, if we wanted to know about the content of a trial, reading the trial transcript would allow us to form our own opinion 'first-hand', as opposed to hearing a reporter's 'second-hand' overview of what went on. See *Secondary source* for a comparison.

Probability As researchers in psychology we want to draw conclusions from our analyses about all sorts of things of psychological

Figure 33 Primary source

interest—is there a relationship between age and memory, are there really gender differences in leadership ability, why do some students appear not to love research methods classes (!) etc.? When we test our *sample* of participants we want to be able to generalize our conclusions to the larger *population* of interest, and we do this using *inferential* tests (or tests that allow us to infer things about our population). But we have to be careful because we use probability (or the expected likelihood of something occurring) to do so. We can never be 100% certain that the conclusions we have drawn are correct, we can only acknowledge the likelihood or the probability that they are. (See *Alpha level* for more information in this area).

Probability sampling Probability sampling is a form of sampling in which each *participant* (or case) from a *population* has a known probability of being included in the sample (and also *could* be included within it). For example, choosing every tenth person from a list of the total population of interest would be a form of probability sampling. See also *Random sampling*.

Procedure (lab report) When you bake a cake you need to know the ingredients and the method used to bake it. Similarly, when you are writing up your research you need to describe your *Materials* and/or *Apparatus* (your cake-baking 'ingredients' and equipment) and your Procedure (your cake-baking 'method'). So this sub-section of your report simply describes exactly what you and your participants did, from the beginning of the study to the end of data collection. Depending on the nature of the study you may also include some elements of the *Design* in this section. But do not be tempted to include, here, for example, information about how you recruited your participants (this goes in the *Participants* section) or what you did with the data collected (this goes in the *Results*)—just include the information required to enable another keen researcher to replicate your study.

Prospective study A prospective study is an *observational study* which takes place over a period of time (so a type of *longitudinal study*), rather than on a single occasion. Importantly the research question is set at the start of the study and participants are recruited *before* they exhibit or experience the outcome of interest (e.g. mental health difficulties, criminal behaviour, etc.). See also *Longitudinal* and *Retrospective* studies.

Psychometrics This term describes the techniques used to design, administer, and interpret quantitative tests measuring a whole host of psychological variables, such as intelligence, personality traits, and other mental states. You will probably be most familiar with the use of psychometric tests by recruitment firms to assess someone's suitability for a job.

Pure research Sometimes a scientist is interested in a particular question for no other reason than to expand knowledge and understanding in that area. Charles Darwin, for example, was driven to understand how it was that species appeared to change over time and were so well suited to the environments they found themselves in. Darwin did not know how his research, and the theory of evolution that resulted, might be applied in the future, but he did know that the question was worth asking! So pure research is driven by the desire to expand scientific knowledge, not to solve a particular problem. You can compare this to *applied research.*

Purposive sampling (or Judgement sampling) Purposive sampling is a way of selecting participants for a study from a very specific group of people we are interested in (i.e. the *population*). It is where a researcher selects a *sample* based on their knowledge of the study and population (or group of people to be researched) and selects only those who are relevant to it. (You can compare this with other forms of sampling which may not require specific selection criteria, e.g. *opportunity sampling*). Again here, the clue is in the name—participants are being recruited with a particular purpose in mind. For example, if we wanted to interview participants about their experience of living with one of the many tribes in the Amazon rainforest, it would be important to identify people who had actually done so—interviewing any old university undergraduates would probably not be of much help!

Pygmalion effect The Pygmalion effect is said to have happened when the high expectations of the researcher lead to increases in the performance of participants. This is most often linked to the relationship between students and teachers (when it is called the Rosenthal Effect), whereby students perform better when their teachers expect a lot from them. Interestingly (yes, we really do think so!), the name originates from Greek mythology, and is used as a symbol in the play by George Bernard Shaw. You may be interested to see how this term relates to the *Hawthorne effect,* too.

Q-Methodology Q-methodology (or *Q-sort*) is a mixed methodology allowing the systematic investigation of an issue or topic on which participants might take different perspectives. The process generally begins with the researcher writing subjective statements about the topic. These would cover, as broadly as possible, the diversity of possible perspectives on that topic, perhaps being informed by prior *interviews* or media content etc. The statements would then be written onto cards enabling them to be sorted (hence Q-sort) using some form of *Likert* scoring system. The results would then be analysed using by-person *factor analysis*⋆ in order to uncover the underlying *factors* of the topic. As such it is a *mixed methodology* employing both *qualitative* (interviews, researcher judgement on the development of the statements) and *quantitative* (factor analysis) elements.

As an example, an evolutionary psychologist might want to investigate gender differences in requirements of a long-term partner. They might ask men and women to rank a set of statements about the importance of, let's say, kindness, earning power, status, attractiveness, and so on from most to least important. The results could then be analysed to see how men and women differ in their expectations of a long-term partner.

For the very interested, there are two types of factor analysis. The 'typical' factor analysis ('R') sorts by *variable*, not person. 'Q' factor analysis, however, sorts by person, not by variable. In other words, 'Q' looks for *correlations* between participants across variables (whereas 'R' looks for correlations between variables across participants), and it is this sort of analysis that gives the letter 'Q' to Q-methodology.

Q-sort—see *Q-methodology*

Quadratic trend A lot of the analyses we conduct in psychology rely on the assumption that the data will form a linear pattern—a straight line when plotted on a graph. But not all data follow this pattern. When the data have a single bend, either upwards or downwards, it is called a quadratic trend. The Yerkes Dodson curve is a well-known example of this and is named after, you've guessed it, Robert Yerkes and John Dodson and their research into the relationship between arousal and performance. Compare the Quadratic trend with a '*linear trend*', '*cubic trend*', and '*quartic trend*'. See *Trend analysis* for diagrams.

Yerkes, R.M., & Dodson, J.D. (1908). The relation of strength of stimulus to rapidity of habit-formation. *Journal of Comparative Neurology and Psychology. 18*, 459–82. doi:10.1002/cne.920180503

Qualitative data—see *Qualitative research*

Qualitative research Qualitative research methods rely, not surprisingly, on qualitative data. The data are not numerical but come instead in the form of words, texts, symbols etc. and may be drawn from data collection methods including *interviews, focus groups, observations* and so on. Analyses are not statistical but might involve the analysis of themes emerging from transcripts or images, the nuances of conversation and so on. Qualitative research tends to be used more in the social sciences, and in terms of psychology, more in certain sub-disciplines (e.g. social and developmental psychology) than in other sub-disciplines (e.g. cognitive psychology and biopsychology). It is generally compared to *quantitative research methods*.

Quantile Used in probability theory, quantiles are special 'cut points' which divide a ranked dataset into groups of equal sizes. The number of quantiles is always one less than the number of groups produced. For example, if you want to have three equally sized groups in a dataset, you will need two cut points or quantiles. Interestingly (?!), many of the commonly used quantiles have their own name. For two groups, the one quantile is called the *median*. For three groups the quantiles are called tertiles, for four, *quartiles* and so on.

Quantitative data These are numerical data that are collected when you use a *quantitative research* approach. See *levels of measurement* for different types of data that can be collected.

Quantitative research If you like numbers you'll like quantitative research methods. This is because quantitative research is based on numerical data, and what you do with them will involve numerical calculations. For example, if you want to compare men and women on leadership ability, your variables would be coded and recorded numerically (e.g. for gender, men might be coded as '1' and women '2', and for leadership ability, data might be collected through a questionnaire from which you might calculate a leadership score from a totalled number of items using a *Likert scale*). You would then carry out a statistical, numerical analysis to see whether there is, in fact, a *significant* gender

difference. Quantitative research methods are used in the hard sciences (e.g. chemistry, physics, and biology) so it shouldn't be a surprise that they tend to have been adopted in psychology generally, and particularly at the 'harder' end of psychology, for example in cognitive psychology and biopsychology. Quantitative research methods are generally contrasted with *qualitative research methods*.

Quartic trend A lot of the analyses we conduct in psychology assume that the data will form a linear pattern—a straight line when plotted on a graph. But not all data follow this pattern. When the data have three changes in direction, either upwards or downwards, it is called a quartic trend. Compare this with a '*linear trend*', '*quadratic trend*', and '*cubic trend*'. See *Trend analysis* for diagrams.

Quartiles Used when describing data, the quartiles of a ranked dataset represent three cut-points in the data, splitting the dataset neatly into four equally sized groups. This can be seen clearly in a *boxplot* (see Figure 7) in which the *interquartile range* (or middle two quarters of the dataset), is evident. The three quartiles are the upper and lower edge of the box (if presented vertically) and the line which appears within the box (which represents the *median* or middle score). Be careful not to confuse quartiles with *quantiles*—similar but not the same!

Quasi experiment This is a type of research design where the researcher is unable to randomly assign participants to the experimental groups under consideration. For example, a researcher might be interested in the effect of birth order on academic performance. They would not be able to randomly assign participants to different groups in this case as the order of birth is pre-determined. However, having established the groups, the experiment can then be conducted as if for a *true experiment*.

Questionnaire Psychologists sometimes want to collect data by conducting surveys. The questionnaire is the tool used to do so, and is a set of questions (usually referred to as *questionnaire items*) with, importantly, all relating to the central topic or theme of that survey or statistical study (so not simply a range of demographic questions!). For example, Clough, Earle, and Sewell (2002) devised the 48-item Mental Toughness Questionnaire—48 (or MTQ48)—whereby the total of the scores for the items (e.g. 'Challenges usually bring out the best in me' and 'I generally feel in control') allowed them to understand mental toughness in a sports psychology context.

Clough, P. J., Earle, K., and Sewell, D. (2002) Mental toughness: the concept and its measurement. In I. Cockerill (Ed.), *Solutions in sport psychology* (pp. 32–43). London: Thomson.

Questionnaire item A questionnaire usually has a number of 'questions' to be answered which relate to the topic or theme of interest. So why don't we just call them questions? Well, that's a good question (Ha ha) and the answer is simply because some 'questions' aren't questions at all! For example, you might have a *Likert scale* which asks people to rate from 1 to 5 how much they agree with a particular 'statement', or they might be asked to 'tick the option which is most like you'. Neither of these are 'questions' in the true sense of the word.

Quota sampling Quota sampling is a method used to gather participants for a research study. By using this approach the researcher ends up with a very custom-made sample in which the key characteristics or traits of the sample are proportionally representative of the population as a whole. For example, a researcher might want to interview both older (60+) and younger (under 30) men and women regarding their attitude to single parent families. If the percentage of women in the population who were over 60 was 55% and the percentage of men in the population who were over 60 was 45%, then this is the ratio that would be selected for their study. However, it is important to note that some important characteristics may be missed using this approach, e.g. in the study mentioned here, culture, level of education, etc. are not considered.

Q

r This is the symbol used to represent the value of the *correlation* between two variables ('*bivariate correlation*') in a *Pearson correlation*. It will be a number between −1 and +1, and the closer the number gets towards zero, the weaker the relationship is likely to be. See also *Correlation coefficient*.

R This is the symbol used to represent the value of the *correlation* between two variables in a multiple *correlation*. It will be a number between -1 and +1, and the closer the number gets towards zero, the weaker the relationship is likely to be. See also *Correlation coefficient*.

R^2 R^2 or *R*-squared is a measure of the goodness-of-fit in a *linear regression*, so it shows how much of the *variance*, or spread of scores, in the *criterion variable* (or *dependent variable*) can be explained or predicted by the *predictor variable* (or *independent variable*). In other words, does the analysis do a good job in predicting variance in the criterion variable? Conveniently the strength of that relationship is measured using a 0–100% scale: the higher the percentage the greater the variance in the criterion variable explained by the predictor variable. It is also known as the 'coefficient of determination' or the 'coefficient of multiple determination' in *multiple regressions*, and is like *eta squared* in *ANOVAs*.

r_s—see *Spearman's correlation coefficient*

Random allocation When we are assigning participants to a condition in a study (e.g. either an image linking or rehearsal condition in a memory study), we need to reduce the risk of creating biases, and one way we can do this is by making sure that each participant has an equal chance of being allocated to any or either condition of the study. In other words, participants are assigned to their condition by chance. Random allocation is a prerequisite of a 'true' *experiment* whereas in a *quasi experiment* the participants come 'pre-allocated', which is why in this situation it is called a 'quasi experiment'.

Random error—see *Error variance*

Random sampling Random sampling is a way of selecting our participants from the group of people we are interested in (i.e. the *population*). This is the most robust way to select participants because it means every single person from the group of people we would like to generalize to (the *population*) has an equal chance of being selected. See how this compares to *opportunity sampling*.

Random variance—see *Error variance*

Range Used in *descriptive statistics*, the range is a *measure of dispersion* or spread of scores in a dataset. It tells us about the difference between the largest value and the smallest value in a dataset. For example, there would be a range of ages in a research methods class, from 18 to . . . who knows? We need to be careful, though, when reporting the range as it can become unrepresentative of the 'real' spread of scores if there are any unusually large (e.g. the authors of this book!) or small scores, otherwise known as *outliers*. In that case it may be useful to report the *interquartile range* instead. The range can be reported for any data set (other than *nominal* data), but is always the measure of dispersion used to describe *ordinal* data.

Ranked data Ranked data are any data that are measured by being ordered in some sort of logical, sequential order, i.e. *ordinal* data. An example might be the rank ordering of five students on their scores in an assignment—from lowest to highest, so if they scored 58, 65, 42, 52, and 75, rank ordering them would be 42, 52, 58, 65, and 75.

Ratio data Ratio data is a level of measurement (or a means of measuring data) alongside nominal (categorical), ordinal (ordered), and interval data (data that have been measured on a continuum of equal intervals). It is most like interval data in that it has also been measured on a continuum of equal intervals—this is why both are sometimes grouped and called continuous data. Unlike interval data, however, ratio data has a meaningful zero. Let's take an example. When we measure response time it might take someone (you) ten milliseconds to respond whereas it might take someone else (me) twenty milliseconds to respond. It makes sense that it has taken me twice as long to respond because my response time was twice yours. However, our super-quick friend responded in zero milliseconds (how did they do that?!)—in other words, it took no time to respond. This is ratio data; note that there can't be any negative scores!

> **Student Says . . . How do I remember the difference between interval and ratio level data? Ratio ends in an o, so ratio level of measurement is the one with the meaningful zero.**

Ratio variable A ratio variable uses data that have been measured on a continuum of equal intervals, which also has a meaningful zero. Height would be an example of a ratio variable

as a measure of a centimetre or an inch is on a continuum of equal intervals: if John is 6′3″ tall and Sid is 6′2″ tall, whereas Matilda is 5′8″ tall and Sundas 5′7″ tall, we know that John is the same amount taller than Sid as Matilda is than Sundas. Note that for this type of variable there can't be any negative scores!

Realism Realism is a way of understanding the world, or a source of knowledge about the world, which is based on the principle that there is an external or 'real' world 'out there' which can be understood by us, and it is for our research to 'expose' it. You can call it both an ontological and an epistemological approach: ontological because that is the philosophical study of the nature of being or reality, and epistemological because that is the study or theory of knowledge. (Have a look, too, at *Positivism* for more in this area!)

References (lab report) References are provided at the end of a research report and allow the reader to locate the source of the information provided in the main body of the report. For example, if a research paper states that 'in order to understand the relationship between emotion and speech you must have appropriate methods to describe emotion (Cowie & Cornelius, 2003)', the reader can then go to the reference list at the end of the paper to get the full reference. This would then allow them to find and read that paper if they were so inclined (see below if that has piqued your interest!). There are a number of referencing systems, the APA referencing system being the most commonly used in psychology.

Reflexivity Reflexivity is a process used by qualitative researchers whereby they 'question' their own beliefs and practices, in order to acknowledge ways in which 'being them' might influence the research they are involved in. The subjective nature of qualitative research makes this an important element to consider, as each researcher's background and beliefs about the world could influence the methods they use and the meaning they subsequently take from the findings. For example, a white, male, middle-aged researcher might have a very different approach to, and understanding of child care, compared to a young, black female researcher.

R

Cowie, R. & Cornelius, R.R. (2003). Describing the emotional states that are expressed in speech. *Speech Communication*, 40, 5–32.

Regression analysis This is a statistical technique that allows us to explain differences found for scores in a *dependent variable* based on information about one or more *independent variables*. Because it uses variables to predict results we generally use the terms *predictor variable* (the IV) and *outcome* or *criterion variable* (the DV). For example, a researcher might want to know what is the best predictor of psychological well-being. To investigate this, having measured psychological well-being, they could just use a measure of stress as a predictor (*simple regression*) or might also recognize that psychological well-being is a pretty complex construct, so could also include measures of resilience, self-esteem, and optimism as well (*multiple regression*). In both cases the change in scores for psychological well-being (the outcome variable) might be associated with each one-unit change in the predictor variable(s). See also *Logistic regression.*

Regression coefficient In *regression analysis* the regression coefficient is a number that not only tells us about the strength and relationship between the *outcome variable* and the *predictor variable(s)*, but also shows how much a unit change in the *predictor variable* is associated with changes in the *outcome variable*. In a *simple regression*, the prediction is based on just one variable, so the regression coefficient is like a *correlation coefficient* and is a number which falls between −1 and +1 (just like it does for a correlation coefficient), but in a *multiple regression* the prediction is based on several variables, and the number can be greater than +/−1.

Regression line This is the straight line drawn on a *scatterplot* that represents the best summary of the relationship between the *outcome* and *predictor variables* (see *Line of best fit*). It allows us to see what the predicted value of one variable would be, given the value of another variable. For example, Figure 34 suggests that a height of 180cms would predict a weight of 84kg.

Figure 34 Regression line

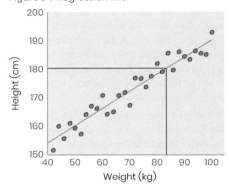

Related design—see *Within-groups design*

Related factorial design Your starting point here is to look at *factorial design*. The key point about a related factorial design is that the same group of participants will provide data in all conditions of the experiment. You might want to see *within-groups design.*

Related t-test—see *Paired samples t-test*

Relationship A statistical relationship requires that a change in one *variable* is seen at the same time as a systematic change in another variable because in some way they are linked to each other. This does not mean that one causes the other, however. There might, for instance, be a relationship between hair length and exam success. That doesn't mean that growing your hair results in exam success (oh that it did!), but in some way those two variables are positively linked—there is a *correlation* between them. (If you are thinking that this is an entirely bizarre example, by the way, think sex . . .)

Relativism Relativism is the philosophical position that a 'truth' can't exist in any 'absolute' form—it can only exist within some context. One often cited example is that 'beauty is in the eye of the beholder'. This is a relativist view as it says that there isn't such a thing as beauty in and of itself, it instead relies on the context (in this case the beholder, the person who is assessing the other's beauty). Scientists, of course, would argue with this as they believe that scientific knowledge should be independent of any individual's beliefs, opinions, or understanding, as influenced by their own personal background. Let's take the example of 'criminal behaviour'. A relativist would argue that what is regarded as 'criminal behaviour' is a product of the time and place we live in—it has no real 'essence' of its own. If you're interested in this, check out *constructivism* too—a similar but not identical philosophical position.

Reliability When we conduct our research it is important that the tool we are using to collect our data is consistent and that it always measures the same thing in the same (or a very similar way).

For example, if you get on your bathroom scales and they tell you that you weigh 9 stones, then, having left the room for just five minutes, you get on them again and they tell you that you weigh 10 stones, the scales are not consistent or reliable. If, however, your weight is recorded as the same (or similar) each time you check (and assuming that your weight hasn't actually changed) then the scales are reliable, i.e. consistent over time. Have a look at the relationship with *validity*.

Repeated (measures) ANOVA This is a statistical technique that allows us to test for differences in the same participants, either in one *variable* with three or more *levels* (e.g. social anxiety at Time 1, Time 2, and Time 3) or when there are two or more variables (known as *factors*) *and* multiple levels all at the same time (e.g. social anxiety and self-esteem at Time 1, Time 2, and Time 3). A repeated ANOVA refers, then, to the fact that it is the same participants in different conditions.

Repeated measures design—see *Within-groups design*

Repeated measures t-test—see *Paired samples t-test*

Repeated t-test—see *Paired samples t-test*

Replication In *quantitative* research it is important that researchers are able to reproduce, or replicate, studies in order to see whether the findings of those studies can be generalized to different groups of people (*populations*) or to different settings, as well as to check that findings could not have been more reasonably explained by other factors (or *extraneous variables*).

An example of a replication could be in social psychology to see if the 'Mozart Effect' (a study which suggests that listening to Mozart's music improves short-term ability to perform certain forms of spatial awareness tasks) exists within different groups of participants, maybe infants, 'university aged' students, and the elderly. So replication is simply another word for the reproduction or repetition of a study.

Rauscher, F. H., Shaw, G. L., & Ky, C. N. (1993). Music and spatial task performance. *Nature*, 365 (6447), 611. doi:10.1038/365611a0.

Representative sample—see *Sample*

Research question A research question is the focus of any *qualitative* study, posed, as the name suggests, as a question. This tends to be a bit 'looser' than a research *hypothesis* (which is associated with *quantitative* research) which instead makes a formalized prediction about the outcome of the research based on prior theory and literature. Having said that, a research question is just as important as a research hypothesis as it ensures that the researcher has a clear idea, all the way through the process, about what they are investigating. An example of a research question could be something like, 'What is the experience of an individual transitioning from primary to secondary school?'

Residual—see *Error variance*

Residual sum of squares The *residual sum of squares* is a measure of how much variation in the *dependent variable* was *not* explained by your model. The smaller the residual sum of squares, the better your model fits the data. You might also want to see *explained sum of squares*.

Results (lab report) The results section is the section of a research report where you provide a concise summary of your collected data and, where appropriate, provide the statistical outcome of the analyses conducted. Importantly, you do not interpret your findings or their implications here—that is for the *Discussion* section. In quantitative studies you would need to report the analysis used (providing a justification for the statistical procedure only when the appropriateness may be questioned by an authority in the area—in other words, you can assume that the commonly used statistical

R

procedures taught at undergraduate level should not need any further justification for their use). In qualitative studies, however, it *is* customary to explain why you used the type of analysis employed. There are protocols for reporting different statistical analyses and for producing appropriate tables and Figures which are too lengthy to cover here, but for more information you can check out the Publication Manual of the American Psychological Association. A couple of last comments: you should not include raw data unless you are reporting a single *case study*, and your reporting of the actual results should include all relevant information, however uncomfortable that might be! (Don't be tempted to exclude those bits that didn't quite conform to expectation!)

American Psychological Association. (2010). *Publication manual of the American Psychological Association.* (6th ed.). Washington, DC: American Psychological Association.

Retrospective study As the name suggests, in a retrospective study the outcome of interest to the researcher has already happened, and the researcher investigates possible relationships or associations between this outcome and other potentially linked factors. Because the researcher doesn't control any of this, causal statements can't be made, but the research can still be useful. For example, medical research might use a retrospective study to look at the risk factors associated with heart disease or diabetes by looking for differences between those who present with heart disease or diabetes and those who don't.

Right to withdraw As an ethical concept this means that anyone taking part in a study has the right to stop participating at any time, without needing to offer a reason why. This option should always be pointed out to participants at the start of any research and again during the research should the participant look agitated or distressed. Participants also have the right to have any data they might have provided removed from the study (although this is often subject to a specific time frame, e.g. up to the point of data analysis and may be difficult where data have been anonymized).

Rosenthal effect—see *Pygmalion effect*

Rotation In relation to *factor analysis*, rotation is a process used to help make it easier for the underlying *factors* in the data to be understood. Essentially it tries to find the best fit between each variable and the underlying factors either by clustering those that correlate well together (*oblique rotation*) or by separating those that don't (*orthogonal rotation*)! So, oblique rotation and orthogonal rotation are the two main types of rotation used.

Roy's largest root This is one of the *multivariate* test statistics that might be reported when conducting *MANOVA*. It is one of a number of multivariate statistics (see list at end of definition) and it simply tells us whether the groups in our analysis are significantly different or not (using *eigenvalues* to do so). However, Roy's largest root is affected by *platykurtic* distributions, so you need to look at the distribution of your data carefully to see if it's appropriate. The test statistic is always less than or equal to Hotelling's trace, but the larger the value, the more likely it is that there is a significant difference between the groups being tested. See also *Hotelling's T²*, *Pillai Bartlett trace*, and *Wilks's lambda* for alternative statistics.

R

σ Lowercase sigma is the symbol used for Standard deviation (as are *SD, Sd* and *s*).

S—see *Standard deviation*

Sample Although, when we are conducting research, we would like to find out about everybody in a particular group we are interested in (the *population*), this is generally not realistic, so we have to choose a group of people who would be representative of that bigger group and are ideally like them in all important respects. The group of people who become our participants are called our 'sample'. For example, I might be interested in the experience of all first-year Psychology undergraduate students in the UK being taught research methods. I can't realistically interview all of them so I will have to pick a sample of students from a range of UK universities which will represent that larger group.

Sample distribution Not to be confused with *sampling distribution*, this is the way that specific individuals (or observed data values) within any given sample are distributed. Have a look at *normal distribution, skewness,* and *kurtosis* for varying possibilities.

Sample selection bias Also known as sampling bias or selection bias, this happens when the sample taking part in a piece of research is not representative of the intended population as a whole, providing results which may be misleading. For example, when governments try to find out the results of an election based on exit polls they often get it wrong because the people they speak to are from just a small area of the country, and only those willing to reveal how they voted are included.

Sample size Quite simply, the sample size describes the number of values or individuals in any given sample. A larger sample generally leads to a more precise outcome when looking at the statistics gained from analysis of the data.

Sampling bias—see *Sample selection bias*

Sampling distribution Not to be confused with *sample distribution*, this is the theoretical distribution of the scores or values for any particular statistic, e.g. the mean, standard deviation, variance, etc. Using the mean as an example, you can think of it like this: when we collect data from a sample of the population, the mean is going to vary a little depending on the sample. If (theoretically) we took the mean from lots of different samples within our population, each of those means would differ slightly, and we could build up a pattern of sample means (see figure 35 for an illustration). This pattern represents the sampling distribution.

Figure 35 Sampling distribution

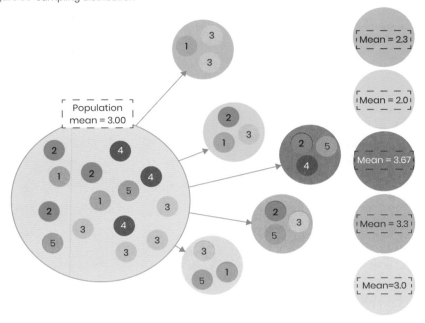

Sampling error This refers to the irregularities that we find in our data due to a sample being used rather than a whole population. It happens at the data collection stage, and can mean that our data do not fully represent the characteristics, qualities, behaviours, etc. of the entire population. For example, when governments try to find out the results of an election based on exit polls, you would have a sampling error if a good range of voters have been approached but only the elderly voters have responded. (If, on the other hand, the people you approached were from just a small area of the country, you have introduced a *sampling bias*.)

Saturation In *qualitative research*, saturation is the point at which your data are becoming repetitive, rendering the collection of more data null and void. Identifying when you have reached saturation is subjective but iterative—in other words, it requires you to collect data, assess them, collect more, assess them again, and so on until you sort of know, as a researcher, what you are going to find.

Scale A scale is an ordered set of numbers or symbols, and which scale you use is dependent upon the type of data collected. To understand this have a look at '*levels of measurement*' first. If we were looking at information regarding height, we could collect data as follows. For *nominal* data the scale would be in the form of *frequency data* or the number of *participants* or 'counts' in any category (for example, eye colour – grey, green, brown, blue, other – recorded using a tally chart as in figure 36). For *ordinal* data the data will be presented in a logical, sequential order but with no meaningful scale between each data point (for example, 'Chocolate is wonderful' – Strongly disagree to Strongly agree—see figure 37). You'll often find this data may be collected using a *Likert scale*. For *interval* and *ratio* data the scale will represent the equally spaced intervals between each unit of measurement (for example, the number of people at each inch interval— see Figure 38).

Scattergram—see *Scatterplot*

Figure 36 Scale: nominal data

Tally chart for eye colour				
Grey	Green	Brown	Blue	Other
||	|	ЖЖ ||	ЖЖ	|

Figure 37 Scale: ordinal data

How much do you agree with the statement is 'chocolate is wonderful?					
	Strongly disagree	Disagree	Neither agree nor disagree	Agree	Strongly agree
Participant 1	✓				
Participant 2			✓		
Participant 3				✓	

Figure 38 Scale: ratio data

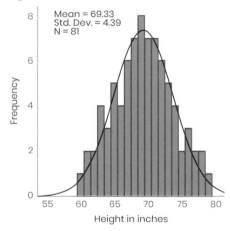

Mean = 69.33
Std. Dev. = 4.39
N = 81

Height in inches

Scattergraph—see *Scatterplot*

Scatterplot Also called a *scattergraph* or *scattergram*, this is a graph that provides a visual illustration of the data used in a *correlation*. Each point on the graph represents the place where the values of two different variables meet. The pattern that these data points create tells us something about the strength and direction of the relationship (*correlation*) between the two variables. The less spread out the data points are (i.e. bunched up around a straight line) the stronger the relationship is likely to be, while the angle of the 'line' indicates the direction of the relationship. If it runs from the bottom left to

top right a positive relationship is suggested, and if it runs from top left to bottom right a negative relationship is suggested. If the data points are randomly spread out, then no relationship is suggested between the two variables. In the examples in Figure 39 the positive correlation between reading ability and age shows that as children get older, their reading improves; no correlation shows that age is not related to happiness; and the negative correlation shows that as people age their enthusiasm for change reduces. See *Line of best fit* for more examples.

Scientific method This is an umbrella term that relates to a systematic method for conducting research. The aim of this approach is to produce *reliable*, *valid*, and *generalizable* findings. It starts with the identification of a specific problem and the formulation of a clear *hypothesis*. Data are then collected (through observation or experiments) and the hypothesis is tested. This can sometimes be the end of the process, or it might be the start of further research, with the hypothesis needing to be modified in some way.

Scree plot This is a type of graph that is associated with *factor analysis*. It plots the *eigenvalues* (on the *y-axis*) against the number of possible *factors* (on the *x-axis*). It allows us to see how many really important factors there are in our data. Interestingly (well, we think so), this graph gets its name (a geographical term) from its similarity to the

S

Figure 39 Scatterplot

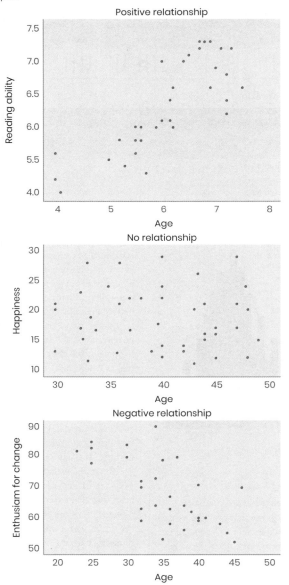

way broken rocks and debris—scree—gather at the base of a cliff or crag. See the lovely picture in Figure 40.

Sd—see *Standard deviation*

SD—see *Standard deviation*

Secondary source When we gather data for a psychological study we usually want to do so using questionnaires, experiments, observations, etc., which would mean that the information comes directly to us from our participants. However, this is not always possible, and

Figure 40 Scree plot

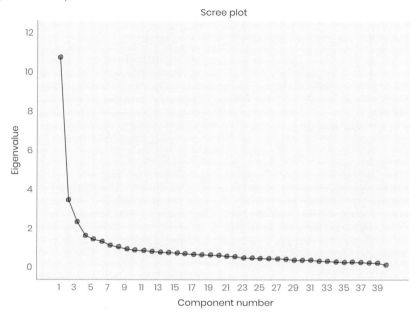

sometimes we have to use or refer to information that has already been collected. This can include data-bases, biographical works, literature reviews in articles, etc. For example, you might read an article by Smith and Jones (2010) in which they have described a study by Green (1996). If you then go on to report on Green's (1996) study as it is described in that article, you are using a secondary source—i.e. Smith and Jones' (2010) interpretation of what went on. On the other hand, if you read the original Green (1996) paper your report would contain your own, first-hand interpretation, and this would be from a *primary source*—see earlier entry.

Selection bias—see *Sample selection bias*

Semi-structured interview A semi-structured interview is one which is based on an initial framework of pre-set questions but which may develop in the course of the interview itself, with the expectation that the interviewer will explore any ideas that emerge from the interviewee's responses. The order in which the questions are presented to the interviewee will be flexible allowing for a more natural flow of 'conversation'.

Sigma (Σ) The Greek symbol meaning 'sum of'.

Sigma (σ)—see *Standard deviation*

Significance (*p*) In quantitative research we use this term when we are considering how important the outcome of our research is. But what we are really referring to is *statistical* significance, because we are trying to assess whether our results are better than could be achieved by chance (it's a meaningful result). For example, if I toss a coin and correctly guess that it will land on 'heads', I've got a 50:50 chance of getting it right—not very impressive, or significant. However, if I toss a coin 20 times and guess correctly 19 times, that would be pretty amazing, and in psychological terms would be statistically significant because it means I was right 95% of the time. As an example, if your Research Methods Class scored an average of 68% in your exam and your friend's Research Methods Class scored an average of 64%, you could be patting yourself on the back—but your friend might well say that the difference just occurred by chance. You could think this is mealy mouthed of your friend, but an analysis will tell

S

you whether the difference *was* a chance finding or not. Statistically, you have a 'significant' result when your analysis leads you to reject the *null hypothesis* and accept the *experimental hypothesis*. Because all of this is linked to the *probability* of something happening, we use *p* as the symbol for significance, and in the majority of cases we want *p* to be ≤ (less than or equal to) .05 or 5%.

Significance level Because data are odd and unpredictable and we can never be 100% certain of anything*, the significance level is the level of uncertainty that a researcher would regard as okay for accepting the *experimental hypothesis* (see *Type I error*). This is normally set at just 5% (so significance would be written as $p \leq .05$) but could be changed depending on the need for certainty. For example, in medicine you wouldn't want to be 95% sure that a new medicine wouldn't poison you, so medical researchers might set their significance level at 1% or even .1%. The significance level is also called the alpha level, or α.

*If you want to know more about this, check out Karl Popper and his black swans.

Sign test This is a simple, *non-parametric* test that is used when we want to investigate whether there is a statistically significant difference between two related groups of data (a *dependent*, *repeated*, or *within-groups design*). It simply tests the difference between the two scores (either positive or negative) and indicates the direction of the difference. In this way, it is the same as *Wilcoxon's signed rank test*; however, the sign test does not go on to consider the size of the difference, so it is much less powerful.

For example, a researcher is considering whether there is a difference in concentration levels—measured on a scale of 1 (low) to 10 (high)—before and after a mid-day meal—and the data are recorded in Table 10.

In this case there is one score that has a negative difference, and 7 scores that have a positive difference. So the sign (plus or minus) representing the direction of the difference suggests that more people have improved concentration after eating their mid-day meal. Checking the significance level would reveal *whether* this difference

is significant or not, but would still not tell us anything about *how big* the difference is.

Simple effects analysis In an *interaction effect* where two variables are working together, simple effects analysis is a kind of 'follow-up' investigation which lets you 'unpack' the way one variable affects the individual levels of another. For example, in a study looking at age differences in two types of treatment (drugs and talking therapy), the researcher might want to know how the treatments affect older people independently from younger people. Or, they might want to know how results of the talking therapy differ between older people and younger people. Both of these queries are addressed using simple effects analysis (for those who are interested, in both cases mentioned here, you would use an *independent t-test*).

Simple regression This is the most basic type of *regression analysis* in which the values on an *outcome variable* are connected with the values of a single, *predictor variable*. It allows us to see how much a one unit increase in the predictor variable will affect the value in the outcome variable. For example, if you were interested in the sort of salary people attract when entering the job market, one factor of interest might be age, and whether or not it makes a difference. Using simple regression analysis

Table 10 Sign test

Before mid-day meal	After mid-day meal	Difference
5	7	+2
6	7	+1
7	5	−2
4	6	+2
8	9	+1
6	8	+2
4	6	+2
5	7	+2

to predict salary (£s per year) based on age, for every 1 year change in age, the associated salary change would be identified.

Singularity In *multiple regression* analysis, *singularity* refers to the situation where a perfect correlation is found between two or more of the *independent variables (predictor variables)*, making it impossible to know which one might be having an effect on the *dependent variable (outcome variable)*. It is one of the issues that needs to be checked when you conduct some of the more complex analyses—e.g. regression. See also *Multicollinearity*.

Skewness Skewness is a measure of how symmetrically a dataset is distributed. In a perfectly symmetrical distribution, the *mean, median*, and *mode* all fall in the same place, and, ideally, in order to conduct parametric analyses, we would like our data to have this *normal distribution*. However, scores can be bunched to one side or the other. Interestingly, skewness is not only represented as a graph, but it can also be understood as a number (hooray!). So, remember, a completely symmetrical, normal distribution would have a value of zero, while a positive number means that the distribution (majority of scores) is clustered to the left, and a negative number means that the distribution (majority of scores) is clustered to the right.

> **Student says . . . The way I remember which way is positive skew and which is negative skew in a distribution is by thinking about whales. A happy whale is swimming towards me (positive) but a sad one (negative) is swimming away.**

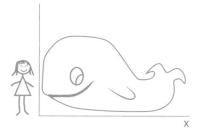

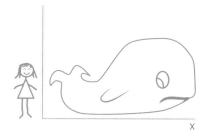

Snowball sampling Snowball sampling is a way of selecting our participants from the group of people we are interested in (i.e. the *population*). We do this by asking our existing participants to find more participants for us. It is a very useful method of 'sampling' as it helps us to find participants who might otherwise be difficult to access. For example, if I wanted to research the lived experience of A-list celebrities I might recruit the one A-list celebrity I know (OK, I don't really know one), and then ask them to recruit more from their show biz friends.

> **Student Says . . . You can just picture a snowball rolling down the hill, collecting people along the way, to help you remember what it is . . .**

Social constructionism—see *Constructivism*

Social desirability bias As the name suggests, the social desirability bias is one in which participants may be inclined to answer questions (particularly in questionnaires) in a way that makes them 'look good' or in a way which conforms to the norm. For example, participants might be asked 'How responsible are the homeless for their own demise?' They may feel 'entirely', but report 'partially' in order to look more empathetic. Issues like *anonymity* and *confidentiality* amongst others need to be addressed to reduce this bias.

Social responsibility This is an ethical principle which requires psychologists to be aware of their responsibilities in the context of the scientific and larger communities within which they work and live. So, having social responsibility means that a psychologist should always be thinking about how their teaching,

S

research, or practice can support and further human welfare, or how it can prevent or reduce human suffering.

Spearman's correlation The full title of this test is Spearman's rank order correlation (or Spearman's Rho), but we usually just call it Spearman's! It is an *inferential test* used to assess the relationship between two variables (so a *bivariate correlation*) where at least one has provided *ordinal data* or where the spread of scores is not normally distributed (see *normal distribution* if not sure). It is therefore a *non-parametric test* which you might compare with *Pearson's correlation*—its parametric equivalent.

Spearman's correlation coefficient Spearman's correlation coefficient is the number we end up with when we conduct a Spearman's correlation. It tells us about the strength and direction of the relationship between the two variables being analysed. The number is a value between −1 and +1, where a negative number tells us that as scores on one of our variables change, scores on the other variable change in the opposite direction, while

a positive number tells us that as scores on one of our variables change, scores on the other variable also change in the same direction. Have a look at the entry for the *correlation coefficient* for a full description. When we report this coefficient in our results section we use the symbol r_s to differentiate it from *Pearson's correlation coefficient*.

Spearman's rho—see *Spearman's correlation*

Sphericity When we conduct a *within-groups ANOVA*, it is important to check that the spread of scores (*variance*) between each pair of conditions is approximately equal, or, at least, similar (i.e. if there are three conditions A, B, and C, the difference between A and B, A and C, and B and C are similar). This level of equality is called 'sphericity', and it only needs to be considered when there are more than two levels of the factor under investigation. You may well already be familiar with *homogeneity of variance* in relation to *between-group designs*, and you can think of sphericity in a similar way. Have a look at *Mauchly's test of sphericity*, *Greenhouse-Geisser*, *Huynh-Feldt correction*, and

Lower Bound estimate for information about the different tests that assess sphericity.

Split-half reliability When we produce a new *psychometric test* we want to be sure that the items within that test all relate to the construct or phenomenon that we are measuring (a concept known as *internal reliability*). One of the ways we can do this is to ask a group of people to take the new test, and then, once completed, compare scores from half of the test with the scores from the other half. A reliable test will have a high *correlation* between the two halves as, if the items are all measuring the same thing, the person will have responded consistently across the test.

Standard deviation This is a statistic that tells us how spread out the scores in any data set are, so it is a measure of dispersion (together with the *range* and the *variance*). It measures how, on average, the scores differ from the mean score of the data set. When we describe our data, we always report the standard deviation with the mean, and you will see it reported in a number of different ways: *SD, Sd, sd, s,* or σ. It allows us to know how good the mean is at describing the data, because if there is no difference in the scores, the standard deviation will be 0.00 (zero), and this tells us that the average score is truly representative of all of the data in the set. If, however, the standard deviation is high then the mean is not a good estimate of all scores in the distribution, because there are clearly many scores that are much higher (or lower) than the mean.

> **Student Says . . .** To help me remember that I should always report the Standard Deviation when I report the mean, I always think 'Mean and Standard Deviation' go together like 'Fish and Chips'!

If you look at Table 11, you can see that by reporting the standard deviation alongside the mean we can have a much clearer understanding of our data than by looking at the mean alone.

Standard error On the whole, when we conduct research we collect *data* from a *sample* taken from a larger *population*. Within that sample, not only will the individual scores differ, but if we collected different samples from the same population the scores are likely to differ between the samples. The standard error is a test statistic that tells us just how much variability there is between samples and how representative any given sample is of the population. In other words, it is the standard deviation of the sampling distribution of a statistic(!). So, ideally, we would collect lots and lots of random samples every time we do our research in order to check the amount of variability there is in our data, but obviously we can't do that. And, fortunately, we don't have to, as some extremely clever people have worked out that we can calculate the standard error quite simply by dividing the sample standard deviation by the square root of our sample.

Standard error = Standard deviation/$\sqrt{N}$

The smaller the standard error, the more accurate the sample statistic is as an estimate for a population. The greater the number of cases in the sample (N), the smaller the standard error.

Standardization Quite often when we want to compare data from different sources they can have different units of measurement. This can be rather problematic! So, standardization is the process by which we convert scales with different units of measurement (e.g. a baby's height and weight) into the same unit of measurement (now called a standardized measure), which allows us to compare them. See *z-scores* as an example.

S

Table 11 Standard deviation

Distribution										Mean	SD
A	27	27	27	27	27	27	27	27	27	27	0.00
B	20	21	23	25	27	29	31	33	34	27	5.12
C	1	2	4	16	27	44	45	51	53	27	21.84

Standard normal distribution The standard normal distribution is a special, theoretical version of the *normal distribution*. It assumes that a *variable* has a mean of zero and a *standard deviation* of one, which means that when the *data* are plotted they produce a completely symmetrical curve and the area under the curve can then be divided up in terms of standard deviations (see Figure 41). The percentage of data in the dataset for any standard deviation can be calculated and, importantly, this also allows us to know something about the position of any individual score within a range of scores, i.e. a *z-score*. This is useful when we want to compare scores on different scales (supposing that both scales have a normal distribution). For example if we know that a baby is 'tall' at birth, we might want to check that their birth weight is similarly above average.

Statistic Strictly speaking a statistic is a numerical value that states something specific about our *sample*. It could be the *mean* value or the *median* value, the *standard deviation* or the *range*, or it could be a *t*-value or *correlation coefficient*. It can be compared to the *parameter* which refers to the same numerical value but for the whole population of interest. Importantly, we use sample *statistics* to estimate population *parameters*.

As an example, an archaeologist might be interested in knowing the average number of fossils found per square mile throughout the United Kingdom. The statistic could be the mean number of fossils in five square miles dotted around the United Kingdom. You could use this to estimate the average number of fossils found per square mile throughout the United Kingdom or the parameter for the population.

We did say 'strictly speaking' earlier and this is because in reality many people use the term when talking about samples *and* populations.

Statistical significance—see *Significance*

Stratified sampling A stratified sample is a way of selecting our participants from the group of people we are interested in (i.e. the *population*). We do so by deciding the salient features of our target population. We then create a sample which is weighted proportionately in every important feature (see Figure 42). So, if I want to create a stratified sample in my University, I would ensure that I have the same percentage of males to females in my sample as in the University (if the whole University has a split of 40% male, 60% female, so, too, will my sample), an equal percentage of people from each Faculty, an equal percentage from each age group, each year group and so on.

Structured interview A structured interview is one where the questions in the *interview schedule* are ordered in advance and each one is presented to the interviewee in the same way

Figure 41 Standard normal distribution

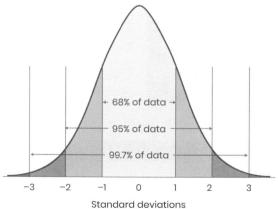

- 68% of data -
- 95% of data -
- 99.7% of data -

−3 −2 −1 0 1 2 3

Standard deviations

Figure 42 Stratified sampling

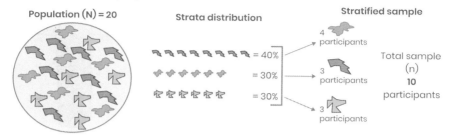

and in the same order each time. In this sort of interview, the interviewer doesn't deviate from this order of presentation, and wouldn't ask additional questions. The questions themselves are generally based on *closed questions*, making this type of interview fairly inflexible, but eminently analysable and replicable!

Structure matrix In factor analysis, the structure matrix is a rectangular display table which shows the *correlation coefficient* for every *variable* (think 'item') on every *factor* in the data. This coefficient indicates the strength of the *relationship* between the item and the factor (and it ignores the effect of the other factors). The structure matrix can be compared to the *pattern matrix* which displays the regression coefficients of variables on each of the factors.

Subject—see *Participant*

Sum of squares—see *Total sum of squares*

Survey—see *Questionnaire*

Systematic sampling Systematic sampling is a method of selecting participants from a given population based on their numerical position in a list. For example, a researcher might want to interview a sample from their population of 560 psychology students at a given university. To do so they might decide to take every 10th person on that list starting with a randomly selected number. The resulting list of participants would be a systematic sample.

S

TA—see *Thematic analysis*

t-test This is an *inferential test* which is used when we want to investigate whether there is a statistically significant difference between the means for two groups of data. It is a *parametric* test so is used when we have collected *normally distributed, continuous* data from both groups and where there is *homogeneity of variance*. There are different versions of the *t*-test which depend on the design of the study from which the data are gathered. Have a look at the entries for the *independent t-test* and the *dependent t*-test for an outline of the different tests.

t value This is the number that is calculated when you conduct a *t-test*. It represents the size of the difference between the groups you are comparing, taking into account variations in the *sample data*. Although there is no specific number to check this against (because the size of each sample will differ), the larger the *t*-value, the more likely there is to be a statistically significant difference between the two groups.

Test-retest reliability The reliability of a measure is all about the stability or consistency of a test or questionnaire over time. One way that this can be assessed is by administering the same test to the same group of people on two different occasions over a period of time, and looking at the correlation between the two sets of scores. If the test has good *external reliability* (and assuming that nothing has changed with

the participants in the meantime) there will be a strong relationship between them. Clearly the timing is important with this sort of reliability test. Test too close together and your participants may well remember what they said the first time, but test too far apart and they may have changed with regard to the construct being assessed. Nevertheless, it is a popular test of reliability.

Test statistic A test statistic is what we use to discover whether our data are significant or not. Each of our *inferential tests* creates a test statistic, so *t-tests*, *Chi Square* test and *F-ratio* are all examples of tests that produce test statistics, and we use the value calculated for each test to assess whether or not we can accept our *working hypothesis*. Also known as the *observed value*.

Thematic analysis This is one of the most widely used approaches in qualitative research. It aims to identify patterns (*themes*) in the data that can then be used to describe the issue that is being studied. This approach can be used on all sorts of data, from interview transcripts to children's drawings, and can also be developed beyond a simple description of the data to a more detailed interpretation of the patterns (themes) that are found.

For more information see Braun, V. and Clarke, V. (2006). Using thematic analysis in psychology. *Qualitative research in psychology*, 3, 77–101.

Themes When analysing a transcript, a qualitative researcher will look for patterns in the data. If something occurs a number of times this could be a theme. A theme, therefore, represents an underlying topic or issue within a text or set of images. As an example, if transcripts relating to participants' experience of being a foster parent contained comments such as '. . . they can be so loving', 'I see positive changes in behaviour' and '. . . it makes me feel valued', then an underlying theme could be 'A rewarding process'. The identification of themes is important to qualitative approaches such as *thematic analysis* and *interpretative phenomenological analysis*.

Theoretical probability Theoretical probability is the theorized likelihood, or the expected likelihood, that something will occur. For example, if you toss a coin ten times, the theoretical probability is that you will throw five heads in ten throws. In statistics we can compare this with the *empirical probability* (or the number of times that something actually did occur compared to the number of times that it could have).

Timeline When we plan a piece of research (perhaps with the intention of applying for funding) we need to have a very clear picture of what we are going to do, and how long we will need to complete each aspect of the study. To illustrate this we produce a timeline, as in Figure 43, which indicates the proposed timing of each of the processes involved in our research. It also ensures that we have considered all of the relevant aspects required, for example, *literature review*, methodology, proposed analysis, ethical approval, write-up, etc. The timeline also shows how conducting research does not need to be a sequential process.

Tolerance Tolerance is primarily used when considering *multiple regressions* and it tells us how much of the variability found in one variable *can't* be explained by other predictor variables being tested at the same time. It is therefore an indicator of *multicollinearity* (i.e. high inter-correlations between the predictor variables—which you don't want!). High tolerance is good, because it indicates that the predictor variables are doing a good job of explaining differences in the outcome variable. However, a low tolerance

Figure 43 Timeline

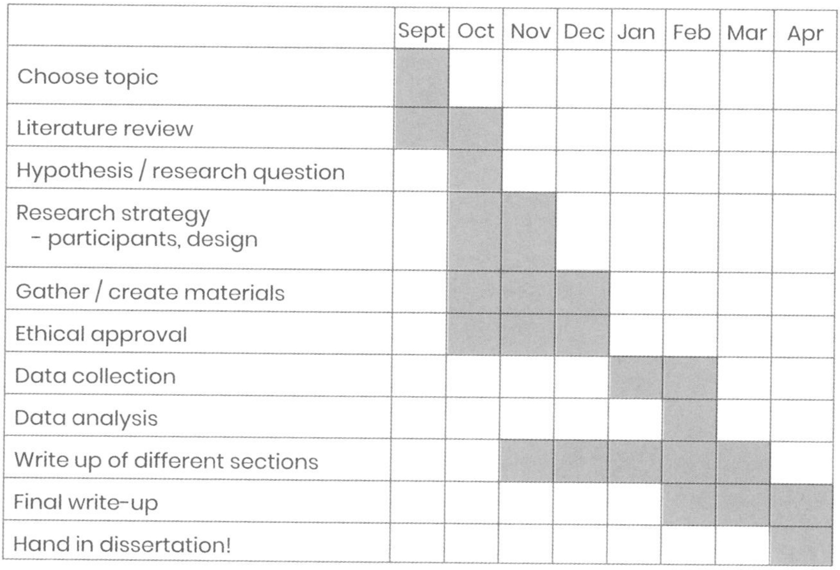

	Sept	Oct	Nov	Dec	Jan	Feb	Mar	Apr
Choose topic	▓							
Literature review	▓	▓						
Hypothesis / research question								
Research strategy – participants, design		▓						
Gather / create materials		▓						
Ethical approval		▓						
Data collection					▓	▓		
Data analysis								
Write up of different sections			▓			▓		
Final write-up							▓	▓
Hand in dissertation!								

(.10 tends to be the accepted limit) suggests that the relationship between the predictor variables is too high, so the explanatory power of the particular variable of interest is greatly reduced. See also *Variance inflation factor* if you are considering multicollinearity.

Just so you know, tolerance can also refer to the ability of participants to cope with some form of harmful intervention, whether physical or psychological.

Tolerance interval A tolerance interval (not to be confused with a *confidence interval*), is a prediction about what percentage of a *population* will lie within a specified range of values. For example, let's say we want to investigate the amount of pocket money given to ten year old children in the UK as our *parameter* of interest, and we want to set a tolerance interval of 80% and an *alpha level* of 95%. Based on the *mean* and *variability* of the *sample*, we can say that we can be 95% certain that 80% of all ten year olds will have pocket money ranging from £4.50 to £5.60. On the other hand, if we were looking at confidence intervals we would say that, based on the mean and variability of the sample, we can be 95% certain that 80% of the averages sampled (so not of all 10 year olds) will have pocket money between £4.50 to £5.60—obviously similar but not quite the same.

Top-down reasoning—see *Deductive reasoning*

Total sum of squares The total sum of squares says, simply, how much variation there is in the *dependent variable*. It is calculated by squaring the difference for each individual score from the overall mean and then adding them all together.

Transcription In much qualitative research researchers will talk to people to hear their views, opinions, or experiences of various phenomena, either using one to one *interviews*,

or groups (called *focus groups*). It is easy, of course, to audio or video record these 'conversations', but for analysis purposes it is useful to convert this into the written form or 'transcripts' for closer consideration. This process is called transcription. For those of you who love etymology (is there anybody who doesn't?!), the word 'transcribe' comes from the Latin word 'scribere' meaning 'to write'.

Trend analysis This is a statistical procedure that is used to assess the 'shape' (linear or non-linear) of the relationship between two quantitative variables. As a lot of the analyses we conduct in psychology assume that the data will form a linear pattern—a straight line when plotted on a graph—it is important to know this when selecting the right test to use. However, not all data follow this pattern, sometimes there can be one or more 'bends' in the pattern creating a non-linear trend, as in Figure 44. See also *Cubic trend*, *Quadratic trend*, and *Quartic trend*.

Triangulation It is not always possible to conduct conclusive research in a single study. In order to address the weaknesses that exist in any one method, it is sometimes necessary to investigate that area of interest using a number of different methods—a process known as triangulation. If the results of the different methods all conclude the same thing, we can be more confident in our findings. A note to self—you might assume that triangulation would mean comparing three different studies or methodologies. It doesn't—two or more would constitute triangulation!

True experiment A true experiment is a type of research design in which the researcher manipulates the *independent variable*(s), and all participants are then randomly assigned to the experimental groups under consideration. For example, a researcher might be interested in the effect of stress on people's behaviour. To look at this they might give groups of participants the

Figure 44 Trend analysis

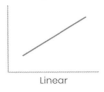
Linear

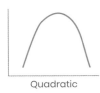
Quadratic

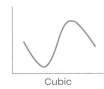
Cubic

same task to do, but the conditions they are asked to work in would differ—e.g. one group would be given unlimited time to complete the task, another group would be given a reasonable amount of time, and a third group would be given an impossibly short amount of time. To assess differences in behaviour, participants in the study would be randomly allocated to one of the three groups. See *Quasi experiment* for a comparison.

Two-tailed hypothesis Sometimes when we conduct a study the existing literature does not give us a clear indication about the way our variables are likely to relate to each other. For example, if we are looking at the relationship between mood and creativity and the literature shows that we can be creative in both a happy and a sad mood, it would not make sense to predict that our results would go in any particular direction. So this means we would have to make a formal statement which suggests that mood and creativity will be related, but not *how*. So our two-tailed hypothesis might simply state 'There will be a significant relationship between mood and creativity'. See also *One-tailed hypothesis* for a great 'Student Says' . . .

Two-way ANOVA This is a statistical technique that allows us to test the effect of two *independent variables* or *factors* at the same time (hence two-way), on one *dependent variable*. Specifically it allows us to look at the independent effects of the two independent variables as well as any possible interaction between them.

Type I error This is a problem that happens when we incorrectly accept our experimental hypothesis (and reject our null hypothesis) when we shouldn't, and is also known as a *false positive*. In other words, it is when we incorrectly conclude that the results of our study are

significant and not simply due to chance. This type of error is the reverse of a *Type II Error* (see figure 45). If we reduce the risk of a Type I error happening, we have a greater likelihood of making a *Type II error*. The risk of a Type I error is increased when you test the same data multiple times—see also *Family-wise error*. You can also get a Type I error simply through chance—significance accepts a 5% possibility that the results have happened by chance, and this could be that 5% occasion!

> **Student Says**
>
> I could never remember which was a Type I and which was a Type II error. But then I was reminded about the 'don't cry wolf' story. So when the village boy first cried wolf, the villagers believed there was a wolf when it wasn't true (a Type I error—they believed something was true/significant which wasn't). But then the boy continued to cry wolf until the time when there was one, and now the villagers didn't believe him (a Type II error—they believed something wasn't true/significant when it was).

Type II error This is a problem that happens when we incorrectly reject our experimental hypothesis (and accept our null hypothesis) when we shouldn't, and is also known as a *false negative*. In other words, it is when we incorrectly conclude that the results of our study are not significant but instead, due to chance. This type of error is the reverse of a *Type I Error* (see figure 45). If we reduce the risk of a Type II error happening, we have a greater likelihood of making a Type I error.

Figure 45 Type I and Type II errors

| Accepting your hypothesis as true when it is... | True (Correct) 😊 | False **Type I error** False Positive |
| Accepting your hypothesis as false when it is... | True **Type II error** False Negative | False (Correct) 😊 |

Univariate analysis This is a type of *quantitative* analysis that looks at the data from only one outcome variable (also called a *dependent variable*), as in the case of *t-tests, ANOVA, Mann-Whitney, Wilcoxon's*, etc. For example, a cognitive psychologist might be interested in differences between children and old age pensioners (the *IV*) in a test of memory (the *DV*). You can compare this with *'bivariate analysis'* where two variables are involved or *'multivariate analysis'* where more than two dependent variables are involved.

Unrelated design—see *Between-groups design*

Unstructured interview An unstructured interview is one where the questions to be asked are not set in advance, so there is no pre-set *interview schedule*. Instead, while interviewers would have a clear plan in mind of the general focus of the interview, they would allow the direction of the interview to be determined by the responses given by the interviewee. The interview therefore consists of *open questions* making this type of interview very flexible, but also rather difficult to conduct.

Upper quartile Used when describing data, the *quartiles* of a ranked dataset are represented by three cut-points in the data, splitting the dataset neatly into four equally sized groups. The upper quartile is the highest 25% of the data, or the data that fall above the top edge of a *boxplot* (see Figure 7)

Validity When we conduct our research it is important that the tool we are using to collect our data measures what we want it to and what it claims to measure. For example, if we wanted to measure somebody's IQ, the test should be a test of IQ and not simply of their memory. It goes without saying that due to the nature of the beast, assessing the validity of the tool we are using to measure a psychological variable can be difficult. You can see in Figure 46 that there are many different forms of validity, and you can find entries for all of these in this book.

Variability This is another way to refer to the spread of scores in a data set. It is the way that each individual score differs from the *measure of central tendency* (e.g. the mean) and is most often measured with the *standard deviation* or the *variance*.

Variables Variable is a really broad term as it covers a whole host of things that we can

Figure 46 Validity

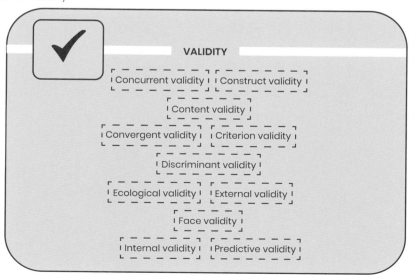

measure or count, manipulate or control for. It could also be called a data item. Examples of variables would include gender, height, speed, position in a competition, exam score, country of birth, level of extraversion, and so on, but all of these must have 'levels' which can vary, e.g. gender can be male, female, transgender, etc., height can vary by centimetres or metres, and country of birth could include England, Scotland, Ireland, or Wales (amongst others!). There are many different types of variables, e.g. *independent variable, dependent variable, extraneous variable, confounding variable*, etc., so why not look them up?

Variance This is a statistic that tells us how spread out the scores in any data set are, so it is a *measure of dispersion* (together with the *'range'* and the *'standard deviation'*). The bigger the variance, the more spread out the individual scores are from the *mean* score, and the smaller the variance, the closer each score is to the *mean* score. To calculate the variance, the difference between each individual score and the *mean* is calculated and each 'difference' is then squared. The individual squared differences are then all added together and divided by the number of scores involved. The variance is rarely reported on its own, but it is the basis of the *standard deviation* (the square root of the variance) which is an important *measure of dispersion* always reported when the *mean* is provided.

Variance Inflation Factor (VIF) In *multiple regression* the variance inflation factor, or VIF, is an indicator of *multicollinearity* (i.e. the relationship between all of the variables). As it is calculated as 1/*tolerance*, the higher the tolerance the lower the VIF, and vice versa. To be happy that there is no issue with multicollinearity, we would want the VIF to be low (whereas we would want tolerance to be high).

Varimax When conducting *factor analysis*, varimax rotation is a common method of *orthogonal rotation* used to identify underlying *factors* in the data. It aims to make interpretation of the data easier by clustering linked items together under separate factors. So it is maximizing the variance of the factors (as in combining the items in the most 'cost-effective' way), hence, varimax! Ta da!

VIF—see *Variance inflation factor*

Volunteer sampling This is similar to *opportunity* (or *convenience*) *sampling* but here, specifically, participants 'self-select'. You could argue that participants from a convenience sample also 'self-select' in that no-one should be coerced to participate if they don't want to, but in a volunteer sample the participant is not approached directly, but decides independently to participate and comes forward to do so, e.g. in response to an advertisement for participants.

V

Welch's F In a *one-way ANOVA*, when the assumption of *homogeneity of variance* has not been met, Welch's *F* provides an alternative statistic to the *F*-ratio. *Brown-Forsythe F* is a similar test, but Welch's *F* tends to be the preferred option. For those who are interested the two ratios are adjusted by tweaking different aspects of the *within-groups variances* (also referred to as the *error variance*).

Wilcoxon's signed rank test This is an *inferential test* which is used when we want to investigate whether there is a statistically significant difference between two related groups of people (a *dependent*, *repeated*, or *within-groups design*). The *Wilcoxon's signed rank test* is the *non-parametric* equivalent of the *repeated t-test*, so is used when (a) is true and either (b) and/or (c) are also true:

a) the same people provide information for each condition (e.g. scores on Task A and Task B)

b) the data being used are *ordinal* (e.g. from a rating scale)

c) the scores we get from participants do not have a *normal distribution* (e.g. in a class test, rather than some people scoring high, some scoring low and most getting somewhere in between, in a test without a normal distribution everyone might get a really high score).

Have a look at *Mann-Whitney U test* to see more about the test used if the design is independent and needs a non-parametric analysis.

Wilks's lambda This is one of the *multivariate* test statistics that might be reported when conducting *MANOVA*. It tests whether there are significant differences in the mean scores for the groups in our analysis on a combination of dependent variables. If you're interested in a more statistical explanation, it is actually the proportion of variance in the combined DV's that is not accounted for by the IV, so a larger variance suggests a greater difference in the means between the groups. Of the several possible choices we have when reporting the outcome of our MANOVA, Wilks's lambda is the most widely used, but see also *Hotelling's T², Pillai Bartlett trace*, and *Roy's largest root* for alternative statistics.

Withdrawal This is an ethical principle which recognizes the participant's right to withdraw from a study, or to withdraw their data from a study, during or after their participation in it. This is generally up until data are analysed, after which time it would no longer be practical to do so.

Within-groups design A within-groups design refers to the way an experimenter has allocated their participants to the conditions of their *independent variable* (see Figure 47). For example, 'type of memory technique', as an *independent variable*, might have two levels (or conditions), a 'rehearsal' level and an 'image-linking' level. The researcher has a choice about how they can test this, and one common choice is to have the participants memorize items in both the 'rehearsal' condition and the 'image-linking' condition, and then compare how they do in these two conditions. This is a within-groups design (otherwise known as a dependent design, related design, or repeated measures design), i.e. using the same participants in both conditions. You can compare this with a *between-groups design* (otherwise known as an independent-groups design or an unrelated design) or the *matched pairs design*.

Within groups variance It would be a good idea to have a look at the *error variance* definition here for background. Specifically,

within-groups variance refers to the error variance in an *ANOVA*, or the spread of scores in an ANOVA that comes from differences in the participants (i.e. the within groups variance) as opposed to the differences between participants in the different groups or conditions (i.e. the *between-groups variance*). In an experiment you want to see whether the between-groups variance is bigger than the within-groups variance. If it is, it would suggest that there is a significant difference between the conditions (rather than simply between the participants) and that the difference didn't occur by chance.

Working hypothesis—see *Experimental hypothesis*

Figure 47 Within-groups design

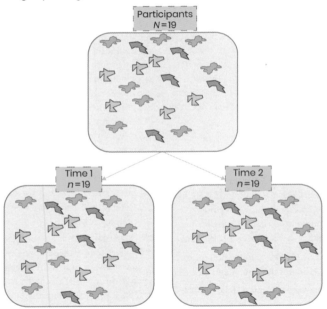

x-axis This is the horizontal axis on a graph. In maths it is also known as the abscissa—you can impress your friends by using this . . . but you'll probably never really need to know it!

Figure 48 *x*- and *y*-axis

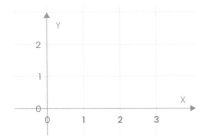

y-axis This is the vertical axis on a graph (see figure 48). In maths it is also known as the ordinate—but (as with the abscissa for the *x-axis*) you'll probably never need to know that, either!

z-score This is a really useful statistic that allows us to know something about the position of any individual score, yours maybe, within a range of scores (the rest of the class). A z-score is the number of *standard deviations* a particular raw score is away from the *mean*—so a z-score of 2 means that what you are measuring is 2 standard deviations above the mean, and a z-score of −2 means that what you are measuring is 2 standard deviations below the mean. So, if we know the mean and standard deviations for any set of data, we can work out the z-score. Because of its relationship to standard deviations it is also known as a standard score. As an example of how it works, let's say you got 65 for your end of year research methods exam and want to know how well you've done in relation to everyone else. If the average score for your class is 50 and the SD is 10, each

z-score represents 10 points, so your score is 1.5 z-scores above the mean. To work this out you would subtract the mean from your raw score and divide the result by the SD: 65−50 = 15; 15/10 = 1.5. If you want to understand why that's good (and it is!), have a look, too, at *standard normal distribution*.

Figure 49 z-score

M = 50
SD = 10

M

65%

−3 −2 −1   +1 +2 +3

z-score

Decision Chart . . . when you have one DV / outcome variable

What are you testing for?	What sort of IV(s) (predictor variables) do you have?	How many groups or categories do you have?	Are the participants in each group or category the same or different?	Do you have parametric or non-parametric data?	Choose this test!
An association between variables or groups	Categorical	Two	Different	NP	Chi Square
A relationship between variables	Continuous	Two	Either	NP	Spearman's correlation or Kendall's Tau
			Either	P	Pearson's correlation or simple regression
		More than Two		P	Multiple regression
	Continuous and/or categorical	Two	Both	NP	Point-Biserial correlation
A difference between samples or conditions	Categorical	Two	Same	NP	Wilcoxon's Signed Rank test
			Same	P	Dependent t-test
			Different	NP	Mann Whitney U test
			Different	P	Independent t-test
		More than two (1 Factor)	Same	NP	Friedman's ANOVA
			Same	P	One-way within-groups ANOVA
			Different	NP	Kruskall–Wallis test
			Different	P	One-way between-groups ANOVA
		Two or more (2 Factors)	Same	P	Factorial within-groups ANOVA
			Different	P	Factorial between-groups ANOVA
			Both	P	Mixed ANOVA
	Both	Two or more		P	ANCOVA

Decision Chart … when you have two or more DVs / outcome variables

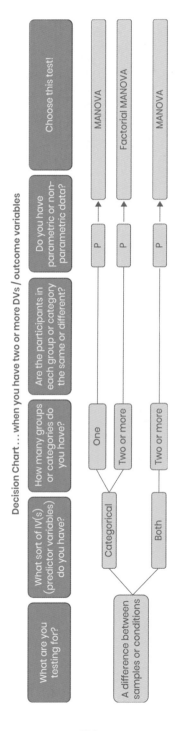

Table A Greek Letters

Upper case	Lower case	Name
A	α	alpha
B	β	beta
Γ	γ	gamma
Δ	δ	delta
E	ε	epsilon
Z	ζ	zeta
H	η	eta
Θ	θ	theta
I	ι	iota
K	κ	kappa
Λ	λ	lambda
M	μ	mu
N	ν	nu
Ξ	ξ	xi
O	o	omicron
Π	π	pi
P	ρ	rho
Σ	σ	sigma
T	τ	tau
Υ	υ	upsilon
Φ	φ	phi
X	ξ	chi
Ψ	ψ	psi
Ω	ω	omega

Table B Useful symbols

Symbol	Meaning
=	equals
≠	does not equal
<	less than
>	greater than
≤	less than or equal to
≥	greater than or equal to
≈	approximately equal to
$\sqrt{}$	square root
x	individual score
$\bar{x}$	mean
η_p^2	partial eta squared
%	percentage
+/−	plus or minus
Σ	sum of scores
d	Cohen's d
df	degrees of freedom
F	ratio for ANOVA
H_o	null hypothesis
H_1	experimental hypothesis
M	mean (see also $\bar{x}$)
MS	mean square
n	number of participants in a condition
N	number of participants in a study
p	probability/level of significance
r	correlation coefficient
R^2	coefficient of determination
r_s	Spearman's correlation coefficient
$SD/Sd/sd$	standard deviation

Table B Useful symbols (continued)

SS	sum of squares
t	t-test value
U	Mann-Whitney test value
W	Wilcoxon's test value
z	z-score
α	alpha: type I error—significance
β	beta: type II error—power
X²	chi-squared value

Table C Effect sizes

Effect size	Symbol	Associated test	Size of effect		
			small	med	large
Cohen's d	d	t-test, ANOVA	.20	.50	.80
Cramer's V	v	Chi Square	.10	.30	.50
Eta squared	η^2	ANOVA	.01	.06	.14
Hedge's g	g	t-test, ANOVA	.20	.50	.80
Partial eta squared	η_p^2	ANOVA	.01	.06	.14
Pearson's r	r	correlation	.10	.30	.50
Phi	φ	Chi Square	.10	.30	.50

Table D Ethics

Anonymity	The researcher does not know the identity of the information generated.	p. 2
Autonomy	The right and freedom of participants to make their own, un-coerced decision about their participation in a study.	p. 4
Competence	Research (as well as services and teaching) are practised within the boundaries of an individual's competence (or expertise).	p. 13
Confidentiality	The researcher may know the identity of the information generated but this is not divulged to others.	p. 13
Consent	Participants agree to take part in a study. They should also understand what they will be required to do, though they may or may not have full knowledge about what the study is for.	p. 14
Debrief	A full explanation of the purpose of a study after it has taken place.	p. 20
Deception	When participants taking part in a piece of research are misinformed about the nature of the research	p. 20

TABLE E

Information sheet	To enable 'informed' consent an information sheet is provided which sets out everything a person might need to know about the nature of the study and their role in it.	p. 40
Informed Consent	When participants agree to take part in a study, they know what they are agreeing to.	p. 40
Integrity	Psychologists must be honest, fair, and respectful in all areas of their work.	p. 40
Social responsibility	The requirement to support human welfare and to prevent suffering within the scientific and broader communities within which the psychologist lives, works, and might influence.	p. 85
Withdrawal	The right of a participant to withdraw from a study, or to withdraw their data, at any point during or after their participation in a study (generally up until data are analysed).	p. 97

Table E Types of Sampling

Clustered	The population is broken down into clusters or groups, a reduced number of groups are chosen for investigation and participants are then selected from within the selected groups.	p. 12
Non-probability	Each case (or participant) from a population has an unknown probability of being included in the sample and might not have the possibility of being included in it.	p. 57
Opportunity (or convenience)	A sample selected simply on the basis of accessibility.	p. 61
Probability	Each case (or participant) from a population has a known probability of being included in the sample and *could* be included in it.	p. 69
Purposive (or Judgement)	Participants must meet specific criteria, dictated by the research question, for inclusion.	p. 70
Quota	The population is divided into specified categories and the researcher selects a specified number of participants (or the quota) from within these categories.	p. 73
Random	Every member of the population has an equal chance of being chosen.	p. 74
Snowball	The researcher starts with a group of participants and these participants then go on to identify more participants for the researcher.	p. 85
Stratified	The population is divided into specified categories (or subgroups, or strata), and the researcher selects the final sample from each subgroup in proportion to the population.	p. 88
Systematic	The selection of participants from a given population based on their numerical position (e.g. every 10th person) in a list of that population.	p. 89
Volunteer	A 'self-selected' sample, perhaps in response to an advertisement or 'call-out' for participants.	p. 96